MW01128238

Narcissistic Fathers

The Problem with being the Son or Daughter of a Narcissistic Parent, and how to fix it. A Guide for Healing and Recovering After Hidden Abuse

Dr. Theresa J. Covert

Table of contents

Introduction

Growing up, did your father ever make you feel unheard and rejected, like your emotions, thoughts and wants never mattered? If yes, there is a high likelihood you were raised by a narcissist, and I can empathize with you on that one. I had a childhood where I was not allowed to do things that made me happy. Being myself, expressing myself, following my passions and voicing my opinions equaled punishment. My father was a narcissist too and it is the narcissistic abuse that I experienced that got me into psychology in the first place.

We can't choose our parents, nor our surroundings when we are born. A child who is raised by someone who has an NPD is, from a very young age, deprived of very basic things necessary for establishing one's identity, having healthy boundaries and self-esteem. These basic things are as simple as genuine love and care for a child's needs, approval of their identity and support, and that is exactly what a narcissist can't provide. Instead of preparing their children for adulthood, narcissistic fathers sabotage any attempt of authenticity. There are very few things that can damage the core of one's self as being raised by a person who classifies as such. Exposure to constant gaslighting, and living with guilt and shame from a very young age, leaves deep scars on a child's psyche and follows them into adulthood until they gain enough consciousness and awareness to heal and reinvent themselves. Many of us who grew up in a toxic environment found it difficult to be authentic and even worse, we thought we were the ones to blame for not being good enough, successful enough or a good enough child. Such children frequently become highly anxious and afraid of the world around them from a very young age, afraid of everyone's judgment, of confrontation, voicing their opinions or saying no to unreasonable demands. Some seek love and validation in wrong places as adults and many feel less-than, even when they are extremely talented, smart or likable.

Fortunately, the great majority of children, now adults, who grew up in love-deprived homes and were raised by a narcissistic father, find ways to heal and reinvent themselves to become authentic individuals throughout life. What was repressed for such a long time, eventually finds expression through self-work and therapy. Such a childhood poses a barrier to personal development and many feel remorseful once they figure out their parent is a narcissist. And that is ok. It is one of the first steps to healing and it is acceptable to be remorseful. After all, this book is all about that, accepting who you are, embracing all your feelings and thoughts, even the bad ones, and then learning to gradually, at your own pace, let them go.

Even nowadays, there is a stigma around breaking free from family chains. The ugly truth is, not all parents are good parents and you don't have to be grateful to your parents if they mistreated or abused you, physically or psychologically. This content is meant to help you break free from guilt and shame carried from a relationship with a narcissistic father. Hopefully, it will provide you with some guidance, shed light on who you were dealing with at their core and learn more about their effect on you. It is meant to help show you how to accept your family history as part of your journey, not your final destination, nor perceive it as chains you can never break free from.

If you are a child of such a dysfunctional father, you probably know what it's like to feel never good enough, even if you are more successful than most of your peers. You probably know what it's like to feel invisible, rejected and anxious from a very young age and you might be far too familiar with how hard it is to even try to voice your thoughts and emotions. Maybe you are a late bloomer like my sister, who was so afraid of becoming true to yourself and independent, only because being codependent is the only thing you've known. And maybe you rebelled against your father's concepts early on and became a black sheep in the family, like me. Whatever your story is, childhood colored by someone's narcissism leaves scars on self-esteem and deep-rooted fears and patterns that make us sabotage ourselves later in life. We are afraid to say no to things that don't serve us and yes to a great job offer because we think we don't deserve it. Both my sister and I spent a childhood, teenagehood and early adulthood feeling guilty for everything and anything, feeling unsuccessful, not talented or beautiful enough, like who we truly were wasn't acceptable. Being raised by a narcissistic father took a toll on both of us, but in a different way.Although we were raised in the same family, we received entirely different treatment. Feeling like a disappointment is not easy, especially if it follows you your whole life. It was a tough road on which we learned to trust ourselves to make decisions, voice our truths and feel good about who we are. Narcissists discard the very essence of their children. They don't teach them to speak up and be self-sufficient, but to stay quiet and obedient.

Know this - you are not alone. You'd be surprised how many people I have met, who, just like you and me, didn't feel good enough because that is what they were made to believe their whole lives. Although not an easy path, because change doesn't happen overnight, a path of recovery from long-term narcissistic abuse, such as parental narcissistic abuse, gets easier with every step you take. I ask you to be gentle with yourself and allow for a change in you to occur as you get ready for each next step. It gets better. Much better. Recovering from narcissistic abuse is something that will make you see how strong, loveable and capable you are and always have been.

Chapter 1:
Who are narcissistic fathers?

P aternal narcissism relates to fathers who display behaviors typical of narcissistic personality disorder. Narcissistic fathers have grandiose delusions related to self, one's importance, abilities and talents, and they impose superiority, are malicious, manipulative and controlling. In dealing with others, they lack empathy, are extremely self-centered, possessive and arrogant, and when it comes to their children these behaviors become even more highlighted. In the core of a narcissist's mindset is a very fragile ego, which revolves around unrealistic fantasies of grandiosity and self-importance. They use family bonds to fulfill their narcissistic desires. Having such a parent creates an emotionally unhealthy environment for a child and leaves long-lasting consequences on their mental health. When such a dysfunctional individual is a parent, the very person a child depends on becomes the greatest source of instability, anxiety, depression and low self-esteem for the child.

Outside their family life and father-child bonds, they are often highly charismatic, charming people and frequently are very successful, well-accepted members of society. A narcissistic father is someone who needs to feel important and in control of everything around them, including the life of their children. They are the people whose rage is hard to deal with, who guilt-trip their children and punish them by withdrawing love, money or other resources children depend on. A parent with an NPD is the type of person who would take away whatever it is their child cares about, be it their favorite toy, forbidding them going out or refusing to support their aspirations. While all parents are protective of their children, in this case, what lies behind such behavior is pure self-interest and a need to protect their narcissistic supply, even if that means doing something that is not for the greater good of the child. More so, the narcissist feels completely entitled to being the center of the family dynamic, demands obedience, respect and won't accept any form of rebellion against their demands and wishes.

While many narcissistic fathers are the overly-authoritative type, narcissistic behavior is not always displayed as openly threatening, especially with the less domineering, covert narcissist. Individuals who display behaviors typical for NPD gaslight, play mind games, act resentful or passive-aggressive, use other's empathy, loyalty and emotions to manipulate them and gain narcissistic supply. They use other weaknesses to make themselves feel important, grandiose and respected and sadly not even their own children are spared. On the contrary, narcissistic fathers perceive their children as their "property", an extension of themselves or a project, making their children feel like they "owe" them their time and obedience even later in adulthood. Such children are expected to live the life their fathers expect them to live and live someone else's dreams (read: their father's).

Highly unsympathetic and insensitive to the child's needs, these fathers withdraw affection, don't respect the child's independence, and are unable to form truly loving bonds with their kids. These children aren't allowed to be their independent selves, or have their own lives, and so fighting for independence and personal authenticity is a constant battle, which it never is in healthy father-child relationships. Their aspirations, goals and dreams never matter and there is no room for being a unique individual. The identity of a child is built to suit their narcissistic parent and match their father's expectations. A narcissist will do anything and go to great lengths to try to mold them to fit their ideal image of a perfect child who admires them - "you must be what I want you to be, or...". They will do so under the parole "I know what is best for you", but the reality is, a narcissist only knows what is best for themselves and that is to keep their narcissistic supply close to them at any cost.

Paternal narcissism also often includes marginalization of the child, dismissing their personal uniqueness and even a competition with the child - competition for recognition, admiration and adoration. Fathers like these need to take the center stage at all costs. Usually, they will live the success through the child and their accomplishments, so they may be the first one to brag about their child's latest accomplishments and make great celebration parties, only for them to be seen and admired by others as a good, accomplished father. Conversely, they will be the ones to criticize and put the child down if anything a child does threatens to crumble their false sense of grandiosity.

In their mind, being a father gives them power over their children, and they think in terms of entitlement to power: *you depend on me so I can decide what you can or can't do with your life.* They need to give approval, permission or consent of everything the child does, from the beginning, because a child's independence threatens this exact false sense of control and power. Furthermore, they need to be in control and puppet their child to be a good representation of how good of a father they are, as it serves their ego and raises their status.

I hope this book will help you break that toxic chain. Us who suffered narcissistic abuse in childhood are those who need to re-educate and re-parent ourselves. And that is a journey we should be proud of with every step we take.

Chapter 2:
Signs of a narcissistic father

A narcissistic personality disorder is characterized by a sense of entitlement, a false belief that one is grandiose, a need for admiration, adoration and a lack of empathy. There are two main types of narcissistic fathers, and both exert these characteristics. They are overt narcissists and covert narcissists, where the first may exhibit more personal dominance, arrogance and extreme resistance to criticism, the second type is more shame driven and less extraverted in their approach to others. Nevertheless, both are toxic and malignant to be raised by, and their behaviors and patterns can easily obstruct the child's growth, causing them mental health problems in adulthood, creating identity crisis, codependency and self-confidence issues. When distinguishing a narcissistic father, there are a few key ways in which one can determine the presence of narcissism. The most important ones to take notice of are a father's attitude towards the daughter, the dynamic of their relationship and their parenting style towards a single child. Narcissists see all their children differently, so it is important to compare the father's relationship with all children separately, as it is not uncommon for them to have a golden, favorite child and prefer one over the other. If you are suspecting your father exhibits traits of a narcissist, here are a few major signs to look for to help in discernment:

A narcissistic father is either overly involved or completely detached. Their involvement in their offspring's life varies from complete possessiveness to absolute indifference, depending on how a child is behaving and their own narcissistic disposition. They are overly involved in all aspects of their lives, from school or university life to socializing, hobbies and dating. Narcissists are self-centered people, and they take their children's success and failure as if it was their own, which will additionally dictate their involvement or noninvolvement. If they are proud of their child, they will make sure the child and themselves are seen, if not, they will completely ignore and disengage themselves from their child's life as if the child is not deserving of love just for being who they are.

They see their children as extensions of themselves. That being said, their children are not seen as individuals, but parts of themselves, which causes the father's and child's identities to merge. Because of that, everything a child does is taken very personally, be it for good or for bad. Every success is seen as a personal success., It boosts their self-confidence and is an affirmation of their own value. Conversely, every perceived failure and mistake a child makes is subconsciously seen as their own fault. In such situations, a narcissist can even rigorously punish the child for embarrassing and disappointing them. The affection between them is present and the nature of such a relationship is a codependent parental relationship. Instead of attending to the child's actual needs and paying attention to their individuality, such fathers live through their children. They pay attention to similarities between themselves and the child and diminish or even punish what makes the child unique and authentic. The father lives through the child, and so they focus on their potential, rather than the real capabilities and desires of a child.

The father idealizes the child. Idealization takes many forms and is based on the father's unrealistic perception of the child, where he exaggerates and tries to boost certain aspects of a child's personality while taking no notice of other aspects. He always has an image of a perfect child in mind, a child who is successful in all areas he'd like her to be successful in and will go out of his way to boost, praise and amplify skills and personality traits he finds to match this idealized image. It is not uncommon for such a father to ignore the child's natural talents and gifts if they do not match his projected ideal. They will push their children into hobbies and activities they personally prefer, not those the child is the most interested in. Every behavior that is compatible with idealized images will be loudly praised, while everything that deviates from that will be ignored, punished, sabotaged or dismissed.

The narcissistic father is overly controlling. Because they are driven by the idealized image of their child, the parental relationship is colored with an extreme amount of control. The father needs to be involved in every decision-making process and needs to have a firm grip on every aspect of their child's life. This includes schooling, career choice, time, hobbies and leisure activities, choosing friends, socializing and dating, personal appearance, money or anything else they can have control over. An excessive amount of control is there to ensure two things: One, to establish a solid narcissistic supply and create a child's dependency on them, and two, to prevent a child's independence and detachment from them.

The father ignores the child's emotional needs. Due to a lack of empathy and the inability to connect with others in a healthy way, children of narcissistic fathers are frequently deprived of true affection, which leaves marks on their emotional self later in life. They are not allowed to say or express how they feel and the free flow of love and affection is interrupted by the constant cycle of pricing and shaming. As a result, such children learn that love is never given freely, but must be earned, which is what the emotional bond between the child and the narcissistic father is built on. Love is always conditional and kids are not loved for who they are, but for who their father wants them to be. Such fathers usually shift the focus to building their child's skills, manners or preparing them for success, completely ignoring their emotional wellbeing. This is why, even though a father may be a present figure in the family, when he is a narcissist a child may feel rejected, neglected and ignored due to his inability to tend to their emotional needs or give nurturing care, just as if he wasn't there at all.

The father displays superficial charm. Narcissists are very charismatic people and like to be admired. They know the right things to say or do to be liked and well received by people. For someone who is not in close relationship with them, a narcissist will appear very pleasant, sociable and respectable. To the outside world, they seem like great dads, who sacrifice a lot and always fight for their family, which can cause confusion in their children - *Is my father really as manipulative as I believe? Maybe he is really trying to help me. Maybe the problem really is me. Am I not allowing my father to guide and protect me?* A child of a narcissist will often hear how great of a father they have, and that they should be thankful for having someone so attentive to raise them.

Narcissistic fathers are easily triggered and enraged. Narcissists do not tolerate criticism or failures. Because they don't have a well-developed emotional intelligence, they display almost infantile reactions to behaviors and situations they don't approve of. Internally, when they feel ashamed, undervalued, rejected and afraid, they will project these negative emotions onto other family members, including a child. These reactions, or projections, can vary from passive-aggressive treatments, insults to outright rage. Because of their mental disposition and idealized picture of how things should be, they do not accept deviations from expected perfection. Human faults and mistakes are seen as disasters and something a child should be ashamed of, not something they can learn from or something that could contribute to their personal growth. There is a lack of compromise, flexibility, and adaptability to other people's needs, including their own children, as a narcissist truly, deeply believes everyone else should adapt to them.

The father makes a child feel guilty and ashamed.
A child grows up feeling as if there are parts of themselves that need to be hidden, parts of their personality that are not acceptable and should be kept in control, including a child's emotional nature, aspirations, interests, and talents. These are usually not naturally deviant behaviors by any means, but simply behaviors that deviate from their father's idealized image. For a child, there is usually an unexplainable element of restriction and extreme

awareness of one's behavior from a young age, followed by a sense of not having enough freedom to explore, be spontaneous or creative as a child. Furthermore, there is a sense of fear that being authentic will incur the father's judgment and rejection. Growing up, a child is deemed guilty by their father for not trying harder, not doing better in school, not looking or behaving better, or not behaving as good as their brother, sister, relatives or neighbors.

A narcissistic father played the blame game. They have an inclination to blame everyone else in the family when they experience personal failure or have issues, be it the other parent or the child. Lack of admiration, recognition for their talents and capabilities, lack of success or bad health are always because of someone else. *Your mother never gave me enough love. If it wasn't for your mother, I would be the main engineer right now. If it wasn't for your university debt, we would have bought a new house. If it wasn't for your brother's disinterest for a family business, we could have grown the business. If it wasn't for your bad behavior, I wouldn't have heart problems now.* A narcissist believes the whole world is against them and everyone tries to sabotage them, so family members are usually at fault when their self-perceived talents and value don't get the recognition they think they deserve. Due to grandiosity complex, they don't take responsibility or accountability for their failures or behaviors, but simply pass them to a scapegoat - a person who is blamed for the narcissist's mistakes.

Paternal narcissism is very complex, but these fathers all display these behaviors to a different degree. Not all narcissistic fathers will be the same in their relations with children, but all of them will have some of the listed elements combined together. Hopefully, these signs were helpful and could give you some clarity about what you've lived through and who the person is that raised you. First recognizing and accepting that your father may not be the protector you thought them to be is the first step to understanding some of your own patterns, behaviors and most importantly, it is the first step to building yourself up and healing from such a relationship.

Chapter 3:
The dark core of personality in narcissistic fathers

Some of the questions I commonly hear from survivors of parental narcissistic abuse are: *Why did my father treat me the way they did? Couldn't they be a better parent? Maybe I am asking too much. Maybe I am selfish. Maybe I am a failure. Maybe I am spoiled. Didn't they love me? What did I do to deserve that? I must have been a really bad child. I am disappointed after all.* These and similar questions naturally awaken resentment, anger, the deep sense of injustice and, not uncommonly, self-blame and even self-hate. After all, no one deserves to be put down and marginalized, especially not by the people they couldn't choose, such as their parents. Asking these questions and feeling every human emotion is ok and it is normal. This is what you need to know - whatever you experienced as a child was not your fault.

Along with Machiavellianism, sadism, egoism and spitefulness, the psychology of a human mind can include another dark trait that relates to lack of empathy and consideration for others - narcissism. Belonging to this spectrum of dark elements of one's personality and a very complex personality disorder on its own, narcissism at its core is extremely toxic for a narcissist's environment. This is to say that narcissists aren't mentally and emotionally healthy individuals and can't provide the same nurturing as healthy fathers would.

A narcissistic personality disorder is characterized by a certain level of emotional infancy. Because they haven't learned to accept and reciprocate affection in a healthy way and because of their lack of empathy for others, they have instead learned to rely on other aspects of personality to survive in society - their intellectual capabilities, physical strength, power, and charisma. They do feel very powerful emotions, but these emotions are usually fear and anger on the negative spectrum, and feelings of worthiness and self-importance on the positive spectrum. Both emotions on the positive and the negative spectrum drive them to do things that would result in someone validating their worth. Their sense of personal happiness, after all, depends on that. More so, narcissistic fathers, as narcissists in general, are fiercely driven by their own fear, and the fear they awaken in others.

Furthermore, there are two main types of narcissism, and these are grandiose or overt narcissism, and vulnerable or covert narcissism. Fathers who belong on the grandiose narcissism spectrum are likely to show behaviors such as dominance, extreme self-confidence, insensitivity, lack of consideration for others, insensitivity to their needs and authoritarianism. They openly demand to be the center of attention, desire admiration, love to brag and are frequently in the spotlight where he loves to be. Those who belong on the covert spectrum, however, are inhibited in their displays of grandiosity. They too believe they need to be admired and have a false sense of grandiosity and an inflated ego, but these fathers, compared to overt narcissists, will be more passive-aggressive, appear more vulnerable and sensitive to criticism. The base of the personality, however, in both cases remains the same. Both types lack empathy and both believe they are special, have an inflated sense of self-importance and dream of being adored, and having ultimate power and control. No matter if your father is a covert or an overt narcissist, you are likely to experience rejection, feelings of unworthiness, feeling unlovable or less-than. The psychology behind narcissistic behavior is such that these people have a sense of entitlement and crave external admiration, which in combination with a lack of care and empathy for others, can be disastrous for their children.

Are feelings of being deemed as unworthy of love and admiration, untalented, unsuccessful, not good enough, and the fear of possible failure something you are experiencing as an adult or something you recall from childhood? All of these are fears are very common for survivors of parental narcissistic abuse. The irony here is that all these fears, however, are exactly the fears a narcissistic father has at his core. These exact fears drive them to manipulate, lie, gaslight and put their children or partners down, only to feel powerful. The narcissistic personality is a mix of extremes, a mix of fear, of not being seen for one's great value, and an obsession over that illusionary value.

Narcissists have tunnel vision and a distorted perception of reality, which revolves around their false superiority and very fragile ego - a bomb that can explode any second you do something that defies to ruin their illusory world. The emotional self of the narcissist isn't built on equal give and take, as they believe they should be the ones to have it all, which is why the relationship between them and the child revolves on conditioning and conditional love. Emotional satisfaction from a father-child relationship, as well as in other relationships in their lives, is established by interpersonal dominance and exertion of some form of power, through arrogance, authoritarianism, manipulation, gaslighting, blaming or lying.

Furthermore, narcissists project aspects of themselves onto their children, which because of a child's innocent and gullible nature, easily finds a way to their behavioral patterns. I spent my teenage years and early adulthood feeling the extreme need to succeed and impress everyone because I wanted to prove to everyone that I am worthy. I thought I needed to be perfect in order to find a good relationship and be respected, but the only thing that brought me is misery, anxiety and depression. In my mid-twenties, when everyone was still discovering themselves, I felt like a failure and disappointment. I really wanted to make my father proud of me. I wanted to prove him wrong and make him see and appreciate my talents and who I am as a person. Narcissistic fathers set criteria for your happiness and because we are talking about childhood, these criteria get very deep-rooted in your psyche as if it was your own. This creates a deep inner conflict and a struggle, to the point, it is even hard to discern who you are and what you really want out of life, without the father speaking through you.

Chapter 4:
Narcissistic fathers and their inability to love

P art of the mental disposition of a narcissist is the inability to reciprocate healthy emotions without an agenda attached. A narcissistic father's love is a selfish love. Because they can't truly feel such an emotion, the love given to the child is always conditional: *I will love you only if you do as I say and behave the way I expect you to behave, no matter how you feel.* Nothing is free and every action has consequences, and so when a narcissist gives, you better believe it is because they want something in return - a validation of their grandiosity. A narcissist only shows attention and shows displays of love when it suits them, to ensure the child will give them back twice the amount of that displayed love. Like in any other type of relationship with a narcissist, there are three main stages they put you through, and these are love bombing, devaluation, and discard. Because of the unique nature of parent-child relationships, in this case, while growing up a child strongly experiences the first two phases, which are closely entwined and don't happen in a particular order. The discard usually happens when a child completely rebels against their fathers' wishes and demands and becomes an outcast that deserves nothing else but to be completely rejected and deemed as unworthy of their father's love. There is a constant swing between being the perfect, golden child and a disgrace and disappointment for the family.

Because a narcissistic father doesn't see their child as an individual, but rather an extension of themselves and a source of narcissistic supply, they give their love based on how well the child fits into that image. If a child is the artistic type and would like to pursue a career in the arts, and their father's dream is for them to become a lawyer, the child will feel guilty for pursuing their own dream. Even though they may be a very talented artist with a lot of creative potential, they won't have the support they need. Matter of fact, they may even be punished for going after the goals and aspirations that make them happy because the only person whose happiness matters is their father's. In a healthy father-child relationship, love is given freely and is a catalyst for personal growth and prosperity in the family. However, in a malignant relationship, the love a child has for the father is used as a tool, a weapon for manipulation and control.

Every time the child does something that feeds the ego of a narcissist and approves of their power, such as listening to their advice, obeying their rules and doing what they find is acceptable, they will get love bombed. Love bombing involves extreme praise, displays of affection and rewards. These are not just any rewards, but those things the father knows the child highly cares about and craves for, be it time spent together, financial support or something as simple as the freedom to do their hobby and stay out later than usual. During this stage, a narcissist will say things that make you feel special, valuable, seen, heard and appreciated, something every child needs from their parents. In these moments you feel very worthy of love and get much-needed confidence as they assure you that you are so perfect you could conquer the world.

Love bombing serves to ensure the narcissistic supply and it is so effective because what lies behind it is a calculation based on careful observation and studying of their child. They know what the child needs to feel happy and fulfilled, what their dreams and hopes are, and so the narcissist will use it to derive the desired behaviors that make themselves feel good - *I have the power to make you feel worthy or unworthy of love.* While a healthy parent will do anything in their power to protect their child, help them build strengths and deal with weaknesses, a narcissistic father preys on their child's weak spots and vulnerabilities and uses them against the child. They know how you react to love so they know how to serve it to you, and they know exactly what they will get in return. By giving the child the power to make decisions for themselves, the narcissist feels unimportant, which causes them to rage, and projects such feelings of personal inadequacy on the one who made them feel so powerless - their own child. As a result, it is the child who feels unappreciated and powerless. Although his words may sound genuine, at the core of his being, he doesn't care about the child's wellbeing, happiness or who they are and want to become. Behind the mask of a father who only wants the best for their child is a selfish, smart manipulator who needs everything to revolve around them and doesn't care about family and family matters, unless they feel threatened. Love is never free-flowing, and the child feels obligated to return the love, idealization and praise. The child will repay them by obliging the narcissist and giving their undivided time and attention, whenever the narcissist demands that.

Discard happens when you, as their child, fail to do what they want and then you are seen as a disgrace and a disappointment. You deviated from the plan of how they want you to be, you don't play the role in society they want you to play and this means you are unworthy of love and support. They will punish you for doing anything willingly and without their consent, by withholding things that matter to you, such as hugs, time, devotion or money. You will be ignored simply for having your own opinion or saying no to something that isn't in your best interest. Cold treatment, passive-aggressiveness, criticism and back-handed comments are something I grew up with. This would make me crave the praise and affirmation I had during love bombing moments and amplify the feeling of unworthiness even more. I would feel extremely pressured to answer my father's calls, do him favors and try harder to be a better daughter, only to end up feeling guilty for not making the man who raised me, my father, proud of me. I used to think I deserve love only when I put others first, as I was so used to letting myself down and trying to please someone, who never had my best interest at heart. I would later learn that pleasing them kept me small and brought me nothing more than anxiety, shame, and guilt I did not deserve.

Chapter 5:
Weapons of a narcissist:
How a narcissistic father controls

I hope previous chapters gave you a clearer insight into what a narcissistic personality is and helped you define paternal narcissism. If your father is a narcissist and his behaviors match plenty of those that were previously described, you may start wondering how come you did not recognize them as a narcissist for so long. Many children, who are now adults, whose fathers are narcissists, that I've met deny and second-guess themselves even after there are plenty of signs pointing out the existence of narcissism in their fathers. They wonder if they are simply overreacting, as after all there were so many positive memories with their father they could recall. This is because they, just like me and you, were raised to second-guess themselves. Second-guessing and mistrusting one's own judgment are part of being a child of a narcissist. Narcissistic fathers are masters of manipulation and disguise. They are masters at creating positive memories, as these allow them to control your behavior. There are a few common ways in which they manipulate and control. Some are more prevalent in grandiose narcissism, and some in vulnerable narcissism, but all narcissists use all of these techniques to an extent, some more than others. All of these techniques are damaging to a child's self-development, self-esteem, identity, emotional, mental and even physical health. They are so damaging because parents are the first role models in everyone's childhood, narcissists or not. The first conditioning and the first contact with society for a little child is through them, which is why children naturally see their parents as the ultimate protectors, the good people, the people who teach them how to love. When a parent is a narcissist, the very dynamic of a family becomes unhealthy and the child grows up in a toxic environment, not knowing or understanding why they are treated the way they are. The very first contact with society is through them, so a child who was raised by a narcissist won't be able to label parental behavior as toxic or abusive until they grow up to understand the devastating effects their father left on their very core of personality.

Narcissistic fathers frequently marginalize and criticize their children. This makes them feel more secure and in power, but it also makes the child more vulnerable to them and more insecure. To feel special, the child in return wants to feel like they matter, and they seek their father's validation by doing exactly what the father wants them to do. Because the father is a respected figure a child trusts, like we all do, especially when we are young, the first thing that comes to a child's mind when they are criticized is that they are somehow bad, that there is something wrong with them, or that they are doing childhood wrong.

My father used to compare my sister and I to other children we knew in means of gaining control. What hurt the most wasn't direct comparison, but a combination of praising other children, while withdrawing praise and affection from us, his own children. *Look at Angela, she is so gorgeous, like a real model! Adriana is such a great student. You are lucky to have such a daughter! That dress doesn't suit you. We better give it to Anna, she is much more developed than you are.* We felt like all other children are better students than us, all girls are prettier and more valuable than us, which is a very unhealthy mindset for a child to grow up with. We were at an imaginary competition with other children, and we felt like we were constantly losing. And while praising all other children in front of us, our success and talents were rarely to never highlighted in front of other people. This way, by using a comparison as his weapon, a narcissist keeps his children small, and ensures one thing he wants the most - the narcissistic supply. Because you are a "bad" child, you want to prove to yourself that you are as good as Adrianna, Anna or Angela, that you are worthy of praise and love, and you wanting to try harder to be a better daughter makes him feel like his opinion matters. You grow up feeling like you are not good enough, so your narcissistic father feels important and in control. Instead of teaching us how to love ourselves and see other children as our equals, all we saw is that they are great and we are not - other children are superior to us. After all, he imagined a much grander future for you, and you are not fulfilling it!

Acting flashy, overexaggerating and bragging about their child's endeavors is the flipside of the coin and another way a narcissistic father gains control. When a child starts to fulfill desires and ambitions of their father, excessive criticism quickly transforms into excessive praise and acknowledgment. Because a narcissistic father desires to be admired by others and in the center of attention, they use their child's success to put themselves in the spotlight and show the world how great of a job they did raising their child. However, they use this not only to get admiration, but to control the child and create memories a child can hold on to any time they start doubting their father's intentions, decisions or judgment. These moments create powerful positive memories, memories when a child feels important, seen, heard and acknowledged. This is how he gains his child's trust and ensures a solid narcissistic supply. These are the memories that keep you, as their child, hooked to them at your expense and keep you going back to their false safe shelter when you feel unsure of yourself. And they will do anything to make you feel insecure and vulnerable.

A narcissist uses these positive emotions and memories to make the child want to please and fulfill their father's narcissistic ideals and desires even more, which creates an endless spiral of feeling unworthy and wanting to prove one's worthiness to a narcissist. When I graduated, my father made a huge event to celebrate my graduation. When I got to a prestigious high school, something that he always wanted the two of us to do, he took us all on an exotic family trip. When my sister got her first and only modeling job, he gave her the permission to get a driver's license, something he would otherwise never do. These memories are rare, but they served our father for many years. Every time we confronted him about something, we'd feel guilty for doing so, even if we had a solid point and a complete right to voice our opinions. Memories like these were a vacuum that sucked us back in every time we tried to break the chain and become our own individuals and make our own decisions. We felt guilty for being disrespectful, when in reality, there was nothing disrespectful about choosing one's own path.

They control their children by being the ultimate provider, and this is a problem that usually erupts when a child tries to go off on their own, build an independent life, move and become an adult. This can be money, material wealth and support, but it can also be security or anything else they can provide, from something as big as a home to transportation. A narcissistic father feels threatened by these attempts and will sabotage them to ensure the child stays with them and validates their importance as a provider for as long as possible. *You won't be able to survive without my financial help; I am afraid it will be hard on you; being an adult is a lot of responsibility,* or *You don't even know how to cook and pay bills* are common comments a narcissist uses when trying to discourage attempts to leave the family nest, as if being an adult is not something that can be learned.

They lure their children back in by letting them fail. The narcissist has taught his children that failure is equivalent to the end of the world, and not a chance to grow and learn; which is why many young adults go back to their families and their narcissistic fathers, discouraged from not being able to adapt to the new way of living, even though growing up is a complex process and we all fail until we learn. Because they don't have a healthy sense of self and are lacking in self-esteem, as narcissists purposely didn't help them prepare for the world of adults, and because many don't have a clear sense of identity, leaving the family home takes many attempts. They would withdraw all financial support if you decide to go and live on your own, but they will gladly finance you if you come back home. That is how the narcissist lures you back in and brings back control over their narcissistic supply - you. You depending on them makes them feel big and important. Remember, a narcissist does not want you to grow up, as that means you will no longer need them and will have nothing to owe them.

The interesting thing is, as much as they create these positive memories, they make them only when they feel like you are meeting their expectations. They will celebrate your achievements, flashily bragging about them only when they are part of their own vision, the vision of a perfect child. Even if I was never interested in medicine and am terrified of hospitals, on his demand, I did enroll to a prestigious medical school. Once I graduated, he threw a party equivalent to an engagement party. It was a huge deal to him. However, once he found out I enrolled in the University of Social Sciences to become a psychologist, he limited financial support, claiming I must take responsibility for my own choices. He never bragged about my success and was a great student. This kind of behavior, when the narcissist reinforces acts and decisions that fit into his criteria, and punishes and withdraws support when the child makes independent decisions, is called destructive conditioning. Narcissistic fathers make you feel guilty for pursuing your goals and dreams if these don't fit into their picture of how you are supposed to be. This includes them not paying attention to or not giving acknowledgments to your talents, and not praising your skills, even if you are exceptional.

You may be a fairly good artist who grew up thinking their art is average. Your father may discourage your attempts to join art clubs or competitions, deeming them a waste of time. You may show them your drawings and they would look at them with a blank expression as if they just looked at a tv show they aren't interested in. If they say your drawings are great, that "great" is not nearly as big as the one you'd get if you joined the volleyball team, something they thought you should do. Narcissistic fathers do this to shape your behavior and gain control over your life and how you spend your time. You drawing some foolish portraits won't make you a better volleyball player, so why waste your time on that? These may be small things, but for a child, their talents being ignored by someone who *knows better*, their father, is a real discouragement, to the point a child may even feel fearful of doing things they enjoy. Children are afraid of being judged, being seen as unsuccessful by their father. They want to avoid being yelled at, avoid criticism and they don't want to experience feeling unworthy, so they fall into the net of conditioning. Ultimately, a narcissistic father does not want you to do what makes you happy, but what makes them happy.

Chapter 6:
Narcissistic fathers and unhealthy family dynamics

Since a narcissist sees themselves in light of grandiosity and the rest of the world needs to match the ideal image they have created in their head, family as the core base for raising a child becomes an unhealthy environment for a child to grow up in. The normal flow of affection and decision making is disrupted and the dynamic of the family becomes imbalanced - the father takes the center stage, the mother, a child, and their siblings second, third and fourth place. Narcissistic fathers see their family members as threats to their grandiosity, tools for making their value recognizable and making their ideals become a reality.

The narcissist needs to be the one everything in the family revolves around, from making tiny decisions to organizing and choosing a lifestyle of the entire family and each individual separately. They create a stage for them to be the main role by enabling their family members and creating a codependent environment.

Where would you be without me, If it wasn't for me you would be no one, If I didn't work so hard you'd be living on the streets now and *You should be thankful for all I do for you* ...are some of the common phrases they use to make family members feel small and undervalued. The narcissistic father has a deep-rooted belief that everyone in the family should be thankful for having them in their lives, and everything that is done is done on their terms or not at all. There is a restriction of freedom and a need not to disturb the waters, rather than openly talk and share feelings, thoughts, and aspirations. The family itself, just like an individual relationship a narcissist has with each family member, is a roller coaster where children and the mother constantly experience highs and lows, frequently afraid of being themselves or doing something wrong - something that doesn't match the father's expectations.

Instead of collaboration, compromise, tolerance, and acceptance of one another, family members often feel as if they are in competition with one another, which is especially prominent in families when there are two or more children. In families when there is only one child, it is not uncommon to see a child and a mother being opposed to each other, all as a result of a narcissist trying to compare, blame and create a distance between them. Using previously described manipulation techniques, the narcissistic father sets the stage where family members are in competition to prove their worth to the narcissist, to prove they deserve love and to prove their value as human beings, as if they are not valuable without their father's affirmation. Love and support feel like limited sources and children frequently feel left out if their sibling gets more attention and affection from the narcissist. This can create envy, competitiveness, jealousy, hatred, feelings of rejection, unworthiness and abandonment in a child who is being ignored by a narcissist, and a sense of specialness, worthiness, success, recognition, and approval in a child who receives narcissistic love. This is until the tables turn when an adored child does something that is out of the balance with what the narcissistic father expects from them. Then, their roles reverse, which further amplifies competition between siblings and shifts the focus from the narcissist's maliciousness to family members themselves. The dislike, jealousy, and anger is not directed towards the father but towards the other sibling, who stole the spotlight from them, so they need to work hard to win back the father's love. Narcissists classify their children as good or bad compared to how well they fit into their image of a perfect child. It is very common for one child to become the perfect, favorite "golden" child, and the other a scapegoat, a bad child, and a constant disappointment for the family.

The treatment a child gets from the narcissist and the place it earns in a narcissist's life depends on various things: how the child fits into the father's ideal, how good of a narcissistic supply it provides and how successful it is in pleasing the father compared to other children and the mother. The family has a hierarchy, where the narcissistic father always needs to be on top, and all other members rank depending on how well they fit into what the narcissist finds acceptable and how much of an ego boost they give him. There is no sense of unity as the core of the family is based on competition, manipulation, and fear.

The mother of a child, another important figure that should enjoy equality when it comes to raising a child, is frequently portrayed by the father as an enemy. *She is the one to be blamed for your failures, she is the one responsible for all the bad things happening in the family, she is the sabotager and the bad guy. It is all your mother's fault. She raised you to be lazy.* Her words and promises are usually made irrelevant, even if what she's doing is truly better for the child. This is the constant scapegoat and an example of how a child should not be, as the narcissist is always in competition for attention and the child's mother is his greatest competitor. Many times, these women suffered narcissistic abuse themselves, they are devalued and as a result they find it difficult to trust themselves and make independent decisions. Their lives, like their children's lives are micromanaged by the main star in the family, who always knows best - the narcissistic father. The mother is frequently hushed and taught to follow her husband's authority. She is expected to be, and frequently is, submissive, having very little power over what a narcissist does and decisions he makes for the family.

Narcissists establish their manipulation and control through relatives, grandparents, neighbors and family friends as well, by making them their advocates. A flying monkey is every individual, part of the family or not, that contributes, consciously or not, to narcissistic manipulation of a father by supporting their actions and ways of raising children. These people act on behalf of the narcissist by reinforcing their statements and behaviors. They are the ones to say things such as - *You are lucky to have such a father; You should be thankful for how tolerant your father is of your behavior; Your father did everything for you and this is how you repay him; He is doing this for your best interest; Your father knows what is right for you.* Many times, people who play the role of the flying monkey truly believe the father is doing what's best for their child and there are cases when they don't have malicious intentions and are, just like family members themselves, manipulated by the narcissist and seduced by their charm.

This is how paternal narcissism takes a toll on children on a much larger scale. Narcissistic fathers don't only affect their children directly, but they affect the whole environment in which the child grows up.

Chapter 7:
The scapegoat vs. the golden child

I mentioned in the previous chapter how competitive the nature of family dynamics get when your father is a narcissist. If you are their child, you could be one of two things. You are either adored, praised and worshiped or you are blamed for everything, criticized and ignored. In other words, you are the golden child or the scapegoat. These two epithets are what shaped your mentality long before you could wrap your head around how negative of an impact your father has on your mental health. Being one or the other is nothing you can choose or change. These roles are given to you and your siblings without your consent or contribution.

Narcissistic fathers don't see their children as individuals whose authenticity he needs to cherish, but he sees them as either acceptable and a boost to their ego or the complete opposite, the disturber of their imaginary authority. Being who you essentially are, your nature as a child, and your characteristics, are what poses you to take on one of these two roles, in the narcissist's eyes.

Narcissistic fathers carefully analyze and examine their children at a very young age. A child's temperament, intellect, character, behavior, curiosity or lack of it, calmness or liveliness are all contributing factors to the roles they will have growing up. It is nothing you chose to be. It is who your father chose you to be. Being a child of a narcissist, I always felt like an outcast in the family. While our father's narcissism affected us differently, both me and my sister needed to re-parent ourselves as adults as we both struggled with low self-esteem, self-doubt, serious fears of abandonment and depression. I was the rebel, and she was the calm one. She was the golden child and I was the scapegoat. And because you don't get to choose those roles, you easily become your father's puppet and play that role without knowing how or why you got it. Not only do you play the given role, but you also know very well what role other family members play and so you play along. So, if your sibling was the golden child, you will grow up thinking they are special and every other family member will treat them as such. And if you are a scapegoat like I was, every family member and many people who are close to your family members will see you as the peace disturber. It follows you everywhere and affects all areas of your life, not only what you live through being part of such a dysfunctional family. Both the scapegoat and the golden child are imaginary identities, not something the child actually is.

The terms scapegoat and golden child are prominent in psychological practice and are often used to label individuals who are dealing with people who are targets of various psychopathic, sociopathic, malignant and narcissistic personalities. The scapegoat is a person who is constantly blamed or criticized for wrongdoings of others. They are obligated to take on responsibilities both for their doings, and the doings of others, taking on burdens they don't have to carry. The scapegoat is the black sheep of the family. A child who gets to play this role is usually labeled as the bad child, the one who behaves badly, who is not as good as their sister or brother, the one who always makes mistakes. You are chosen to be the scapegoat not because you are bad or less loveable, but because you are seen as a threat, a wild child, the one who needs to be tamed, a threat to your father's sense of control and unfortunately, this is what you don't understand when you are a child. If you were the scapegoat, everything bad that happens in the family is your fault, no matter if it's something you actually did or not, and no matter your actual contribution to the unfortunate situation you are blamed for.

Since I was the scapegoat of my family, I was the one who is responsible for everything and everyone. I was expected to excel at things, be responsible, be mature before I needed to be, do things for family members and take care of them, but never appreciated for the things I did. If my sister did something that disturbed the calm waters, I was the one expected to correct that. Matter of fact, I was not only expected to make things right, but I was blamed for giving bad examples, making her do something against her will, and not affecting her decisions. If she got into trouble it was because of me. If a fight would happen, it was because of me. If someone got yelled at and screamed at, it was me. I was the child who would get all the rage from her parents simply because they had a bad day at work, the one to be blamed because the house is not clean, as if I was the only one who needs to take care of the home when the mother is away. Responsibilities were never shared, and while my sister was only expected to have good grades, I needed to do the same, along with taking care of the home, doing chores, taking care of our animals, and going shopping. If I asked for the chores to be shared, I was blamed for sabotaging her, as she had better things to do and work on her talents. That was never enough, and it was never appreciated or praised.

Golden children, on the other hand, live to tell different stories about their childhood. The golden child or the perfect child, although raised in the same family is the one who gets the opposite treatment. They are praised for everything they do, they are idealized, and put on a pedestal. They are the narcissistic father's favorite child. They are the ones showered with affection, attention, love and gifts. The golden child is the one who does everything right, who is talented, gifted and worthy of praise. In other words, they are the polar opposites of the scapegoat. However, just like the role of a scapegoat, the role of a golden child is as equally imposed and something the child did not choose to be. The narcissist chose them. Contrary to the scapegoat who is opinionated, who is considered to be the opposer, the golden child is usually the one who follows the rules and doesn't make much fuss about what their narcissistic father expects them to do. Furthermore, they are reinforced to follow the narcissist and give them unlimited narcissistic supply, because the narcissist praises them, supports them and idealizes what they do. As a result, such children grow up feeling they deserve special treatment wherever they go, they think they are somehow special, unique and better than others.

Siblings who grew up with narcissistic fathers frequently have completely different perceptions of each other, their father and their childhood. While one would say they felt invisible and sad, unappreciated, the other would say they had the perfect childhood, that they were loved and cared for. This is how great of a difference a narcissistic father can make and how drastically different experiences their children have based on narcissistic favoritism. Unfortunately, this difference in treatment not only affects how children see themselves, but it also affects their relationship, which becomes highly competitive and toxic from a very young age. Siblings don't see each other as support but as a threat and rivals. They are opposed to each other and in a constant fight for their father's approval. All children are unfortunately part of the endless race for approval and love from their father. Many times, a child who is the scapegoat has many talents, but isn't appreciated for them because it doesn't go well with their role of being the one who makes mistakes all the time. Conversely, the golden child may not be as talented, by they can be praised and worshiped for the talents they do have or things they are average at only because they are the golden child.

The roles children play are based on how obedient they are or not. While the scapegoat usually has stronger will and is willing to speak up, in the narcissist's mind that needs to be suppressed so the scapegoat is more obedient and willing to cater to their father's wishes. Children are in constant opposition, may grow up trying to sabotage each other, put each other down and frequently grow apart, having a very disconnected and distant relationship. The relationship of the scapegoat and the golden child is not based on mutual trust, respect and sibling love, but on animosity, hatred, jealousy, and distrust. By putting children against each other, a narcissistic father ensures narcissistic supply from all of his children. The scapegoats feed his ego by trying to prove themselves worthy and trying harder to be responsible and mature, and the golden child feeds their ego by being like them, following rules, adoring the narcissist, never questioning their authority and ultimately, wanting to be like the narcissist. Siblings fighting among each other for their father's approval make him feel special and important, which is extremely destructive for the whole family.

This war for approval, the war between the golden child who wants to be even more adored, and the one who fights hard for crumbs of attention, continues even in adulthood. Unfortunately, both roles have their pitfalls and neither the scapegoat nor the golden child leave that war unbruised. The identities that were given to them are false and it is a matter of time, usually in early adulthood, when these false identities start creating troubles in both the scapegoat's and golden child's life. And although opposed their whole lives, none of them actually gets to the top. The narcissistic treatment leaves marks on one's personality and requires a lot of reality-checks, self-awareness and re-parenting, which many children can't cope with. For the golden child, adulthood becomes a dangerous territory they are afraid to enter, and so many of them mature much later than their peers, staying close to their narcissistic father and the false sense of security he has created. Although not a general rule, it is not uncommon for these children to develop narcissistic traits themselves, as they spend so much time trying to be like the father. They are usually less mature, their emotions are infantile and their reactions to not getting what they want are similar to their fathers reactions. In this war, the golden child may even try to sabotage the scapegoat, lie about them, put them down, make them take on the blame for something they did and get away with things easily, something their sibling never gets to do just for the fact that they are the family's scapegoat. It is not uncommon for scapegoats and golden children to live completely different lives, behave completely different and have completely different perceptions of their own family and its members, even though they were raised under the same roof, all due to separation made by their father. A child of a narcissist is either constantly praised or criticized and not good enough, and when these two polar opposites are split between two or more children, his children get triggered into disliking their own brother or sister.

If you have a narcissistic father and this sounds familiar, the sad, painful truth is, it is not anyone's fault. Neither of you chose to be one or the other. You are both victims of an enlarged, hungry for attention ego that got the chance to be attached to the role of a father. The narcissist is to be blamed for the animosity created between you and your siblings, but growing up, it will never seem like it is their fault, because such a father is so busy creating the scenarios where you and your siblings need to fight for his attention and validation. Narcissistic fathers are extremely good at it.

Because they are taught that they are special, golden children are less likely to take on the path of healing, although they need it as much as the scapegoat does. This is because they like to believe what they were told they are their whole life, while the scapegoat is left drowning in self-doubt from day one and as they grow up, they are more likely to want to strengthen and learn to value themselves. Unfortunately, as much as being adored by their narcissistic father makes their life seemingly easier, it can be a great obstacle later in life, when they face the reality, and that is that the outer world does not recognize their talents as much their father did and it is usually in adulthood when golden children of a narcissist find it very difficult to deal with reality, having to be treated as ordinary. Do know that roles can be reversed as the father finds it suitable. The golden child does get criticized and love is withdrawn from them when and if they try to rebel. The scapegoat gets their bits and pieces of admiration when they follow their fathers ideal, but these moments are usually short-lived. The reversal of roles serves to reinforce the narcissistic supply. If you are a single child, it is possible that you took on both of these roles, depending on your behavior.

What is important to know is that neither of them is initially good or bad, less or more loveable. They are just as equally victims of narcissism, although it may take a different toll on them. No matter which role you played, one of the next chapters will be dedicated to healing that is available to all children who suffered the effects of paternal narcissism, as all of them need to rediscover themselves, find their identity and learn what it means to truly love themselves, without the need to be externally validated.

Chapter 8:
The wounds of the scapegoated child

B eing a scapegoat in my family and the ultimate black sheep, I know first-hand how it feels to be rejected by your own family. A sense of belonging, safety, and unconditional love are something I didn't receive. Growing up, I remember feeling like life is unjust most of the time. No matter what you do, no matter how hard you try, your efforts are somehow never good enough. If you do something great, win a contest or get a good grade, you might get a short bravo from your father, but shortly after, everyone in the family forgets about your great achievement and you get back to being the scapegoat, who never does anything right. There you are, giving your maximum effort to be seen and loved, only to get crumbs of affection. This is the pattern that I unconsciously accepted later on, which furthermore sealed my destiny and prevented me from gaining the success I now know I deserve. just like everyone else. It always confused me how people outside our family would perceive my father as the amazing dad and my family the ideal family, when I was living in that home, feeling sad, invisible and anxious every day of my life. I thought, well it must be that I am imagining things, it must be that I am really bad. I was the one who overreacts, who is overly sensitive and who imagines things. Little did I know.

If you are the scapegoat, you are constantly hushed, your sense of fashion is unacceptable, you are antisocial, the weird one, the bad student, the clumsy, the stupid, you name it. You are the one who carries the blame on your shoulder for the things you did not do and things you shouldn't be responsible for. You are responsible for your brother or sister, for family pets and their wellbeing, for hygiene at home, for your father's health. Whatever crisis your family went through, you were probably in the middle of the battlefield, the one to be blamed. You are never good enough, the one who deeply believes that you need to be perfect or you will never be loved. The one that needs to stay silent and tone down the voice if something feels unfair, the one who has no right to voice your opinion. And growing up, you probably wanted to fight for your equality, even as a child, by voicing how you feel, only to be put down and criticized for it.

Scapegoats feel unloved, unseen, unappreciated and unheard very early on in their childhood. They grow up thinking they are somehow not important, and not understanding why. Deprived of attention and loving from their father, invisible to the entire family, and conditioned to believe that they are somehow inherently bad or not good enough, these children grow up to have very low self-esteem, distorted images of oneself and lack of belief in one's talents and abilities. Children of narcissistic fathers are never loved for who they are, but for how well they cater to him, and in case the of the scapegoated child, their father's conditional love reaches extremes and creates a negative self-image, destroys and diminishes the child's self-respect and self-love. Matter of fact, scapegoats find it very difficult to love themselves later in life, no matter how much they have achieved or how hard they have worked. Just like the golden child who thinks everyone should cater to them, the scapegoat feels like no matter how much they improve themselves, they are always one step behind everyone else. They don't recognize their talents and skills, as they were discouraged to pursue their passions or their talents were never given attention. This twisted perception of themselves is linked to poor self-image, lack of assertiveness, anxiety, fear of being judged and rejected, which is how they were raised to be. Many of us scapegoats suffered from depression, as we were made to believe that we are simply not loveable for who we are. This translates into all interpersonal relationships we have later in life. The inability to set and voice one's boundaries and the learned role of the scapegoat, unfortunately, bring more people who treat us just like our father did. Many of the relationships scapegoats have are a projection of their relationships with the father, and so, unfortunately, it is not uncommon for them to end up in toxic, abusive relationships, with emotionally unavailable people who see them as their narcissistic father does - as scapegoats. This way, the effects of paternal narcissism take a much larger scale and learned behavior transpired in all other areas of a scapegoat's life until they become ready to re-parent themselves.

Because you have your own inner guidance that something is wrong or right, every time you felt like voicing it and standing up for yourself as a child you would be punished and made very guilty. The scapegoat is the child who feels the rage of their father while watching him treat other siblings with kindness and love. They are the ones who are ashamed of themselves, disappointed in themselves and those children who feel lonely in their own homes. If your sibling did something wrong, you were probably the one to be blamed for it. A narcissistic father uses guilt traps, gaslighting, offensive comments, and blame games to make you stay silent and stop threatening their sense of grandiosity. This is the child who receives the silent treatment the most of all family members. If you needed something from your father, you probably had to work for it twice as hard to prove yourself to them. The scapegoat, because they have more trouble following rules, are the ones who need to fulfill more terms and conditions than other children. Narcissistic fathers constantly compare the scapegoat to other children, and in that comparison, put their own child on the lowest levels of comparison charts. *Why can't you be more like your sister or brother* is a common comparison and can be very hurtful, as the child is made to feel like they are less than, the less important child and the less valuable one.

The dynamic of the relationship between the narcissistic father and the scapegoat is rooted in the narcissist's shadow side, his deepest fears and insecurities. He not only sees this child as a threat to his imaginary authority and sense of grandiosity, but he also sees and projects his own fears onto the child. The scapegoated child is the embodiment of his fears and as such, it needs to be punished, criticized and rejected. The scapegoat child may be very talented and have a great potential for success, much greater than the golden child, but in the narcissists' mind, this potential needs to be tamed and kept under control, as no one else gets to be the star but himself. This is why the child who is like him and worships him, is the perfect child who gets to be worshiped, as that child is more likely to be his follower and never take on the lead role. Children of narcissistic fathers are either a projection of his wishes and dreams, in which the child worships him and fulfills his ambitions, or his fears, where the child stands up for itself, confronts him or gets to have the center stage. The scapegoat feels unloved and will do anything to gain their father's appreciation and love, especially at a young age, and so they will put more effort into being more worthy of their father's affection. This feeds the father's ego and acts and becomes counterproductive for the child, because the narcissist feels important when their child fights so hard to win their affection, and so they will withdraw their praise even more, making the scapegoat feel even more unworthy.

One of the hardest things for a child to understand is why are they so marginalized and why they don't receive love from their father. It is hard to find reasoning why, despite all the effort to be better, work harder and be responsible, even when some responsibilities are not your burden to bear, you feel unloved and abandoned by your father. What you need to know is that you were chosen to be the scapegoat for a reason, but that reason is not what you thought. You were chosen because as a child you had an independent spirit, which posed a threat to your narcissistic father. The scapegoat is not the child who is bad, less talented or unlovable, but a child who has strong willpower, a child who questions and resists authority and a child who, from a very young age, has a strong inner compass for what is right and wrong. Children who are chosen for this role also have a higher inclination to be highly empathetic, and therefore easier to manipulate through blaming and guilt, as they are more likely to internalize blame. These children are less willing to obey, especially if they find something is unjust, and these traits defy the narcissist and his manipulation attempts. Because of these traits, the scapegoat won't cater to their father and enable them with the constant narcissistic supply by giving constant admiration, so they will be dismissed, discarded, criticized and put down for opposing the narcissist.

A narcissistic father programs all his children to cater to him one way or the other. The narcissistic father wants you to be below them. They don't want you to grow up to be a strong, independent individual who speaks their truth. Narcissists are predatory people and every relationship they have, including relationships with their children, is a constant battle for power where they have to be the winner. Your virtues are turned against you, solely for the purpose of your father having to prove to himself how grandiose and important he is. The programing of the scapegoated child is such that their justice-seeking, caring and empathetic nature is not nourished, but used against them. They grow up catering to other people's needs and in this way, the father's programming finds a way to intoxicate all the future relationships. They are programmed to take care of other people and believe it is their responsibility to enable other people, take care of their emotional wellbeing and take all the responsibility for the success of the relationship onto themselves. If a scapegoat fails to do so, and tries to put themselves, their needs and wants before others, they will feel an immense amount of guilt and shame. They will live their lives trying to please other people only to escape feeling these negative emotions because they are taught that caring for oneself is selfish. Until we start healing, we end up in toxic, one-sided and abusive relationships with selfish individuals, narcissists, psychopaths, emotionally unavailable and manipulative people, because of this false belief that we are to blame if something goes wrong. We need to prove to someone that we are lovable by taking care of their needs and fixing relationships. We become a magnet for people who treat us like our father did because we don't know that love and genuine relationships feel good and replenish our spirit. We don't know what true love is because, in our subconscious mind, we need to earn it, and to earn it we need to put everyone else before us. Relationships end up draining us and only rarely nourishing us back.

Most of these children are forced to grow up faster because of all the responsibility and guilt that has been placed upon them. They believe being spontaneous or failing at something is a disaster that only proves how unworthy they are because that is how they were raised. When they grow up, scapegoats take criticism to heart and take rejection much more personally, for which they are sometimes deemed by their peers as being too sensitive. Paternal narcissism is an invisible threat to a child's integrity and identity, which shows in adulthood, and because it is so hard to pinpoint what exactly is wrong in one's upbringing, scapegoats rarely find understanding and compassion from people around them.

If you are a scapegoat, because you so deeply believe that to be loved you need to be perfect, more successful or better looking , you may find it hard to enjoy life the way others do. You are taught to believe that only perfection is worthy of admiration and that you can't be loved just for being who you are. Scapegoats grow up learning to accept the blame and guilt that was never theirs to begin with, but they also frequently become overachievers, where they are constantly hunting for the next big thing that will help them prove to their fathers that they were wrong, which they don't know is impossible to achieve. And while they are constant overachievers, no matter how successful they become, scapegoats always feel like something is missing, like that success is somehow not enough, finding it hard to praise themselves for all the hard work they have done. Many of us develop perfectionism that is mostly directed inwards. Many take on more than they can carry, take responsibilities for other people, solving their problems and being scapegoats for everyone, which is one of the ways narcissistic fathers deem their scapegoated children to failure. These children don't put themselves first and they believe acknowledging their needs and wants is selfish, feeling guilty and ashamed in moments when they do try to take care of themselves because that is what their father taught them. In adulthood, when the scapegoat manages to live independently, until the healing process takes place and they learn to reestablish themselves, many associate themselves with friends or partners who, just like their father, demand to take the center stage, dominate and take emotional or other resources from the scapegoat. What you've learned by being the scapegoated child is hard to shake off. The combination of pressure to succeed and prove one's worth, while feeling unlovable, rejecting one's needs and taking on too many responsibilities ultimately leads not only to low self-esteem, but to depression and anxiety. The toll paternal narcissism takes on a child is huge, and goes way beyond what you experience in the family. Depression, suicidal thoughts, loss of faith in the world around you and yourself, loss of trust and hope and failed attempts to rebuild oneself are just some of these devastating effects. Scapegoated children find it difficult to heal, because they see setbacks in the healing process as failures, as they are hard on themselves due to the difficult upbringing they had.

Ultimately, as a scapegoat, you feel like you don't matter. Like you are not important. You are invisible and feel like a failure, despite all the success you have achieved. As you grow old, you learn that being raised by a narcissistic father and being a scapegoat for many other people in your life, that the only person you can rely on is yourself. But you also learn that the only person you have is you, which is one of the first steps to healing. One day, you wake up and feel like you don't want to let yourself down, and that you don't want to let a narcissist shape your life anymore. And one day you decide to give yourself the love you always deserved, without waiting on your father to tell you how great you are, and how after all, you are a child worthy of love and admiration. You stop wanting to make your family proud, but instead shift your focus on being gentle with yourself and being proud of how far you've come. Because you have, and you deserve to be happy.

Chapter 9:
Narcissistic fathers, their sons, and daughters

There is an unwritten rule in society that having a father, no matter how emotionally and mentally healthy or capable of raising a child he is, is better than having no father figure at all. Fathers are harshly judged only in cases of complete abandonment and physical violence, and so narcissistic abuse is usually off the radar. Narcissistic fathers do not differentiate their children only based on how threatened they are by a child's qualities or how well the child fits into their idealized image. Besides setting up their children for scapegoat or golden child programming, they treat their boys and girls differently. Because a narcissist wants to be recognized in society, they want their child to succeed and right the wrongs, proving the world how truly amazing they are, by living through their children. Since narcissistic fathers can't build love-based relationships, this inability creates a dysfunctional dynamic in how they relate to children of both sexes. Because their children are an extension of themselves, the narcissist sees and treats them as belongings rather than children with their own needs, thoughts, and emotions. Although children of both sex can be scapegoated or seen as perfect children and both suffer from the same psychological and emotional consequences, the narcissistic father relates differently to their sons and daughters, and the following text will give insight as to how.

Narcissistic father-daughter relationships

We have mentioned the malicious nature of their personality and their predatory approach, where they use a child's weakness against them. In society, fathers are seen as protectors, providers, mature, wise and stable, and this is something the narcissist knows how to use to their advantage. Their girls are not only seen as property but because of the societal image of what the role of a father is, they are, in their father's eyes, easier to manipulate under the parole: *I just want to keep you safe from the harsh, cruel world that can only harm you.* The world is a dangerous place, so these girls need to stay protected and safe from harm where, in reality, the real danger is the manipulator who raises them. The narcissist is a master of disguise, and frequently, everyone who is not a family member will see them as caring fathers who try their best to make a stable foundation for their daughters - they are their rock and greatest support. As a result, their daughters are overprotected, grow up to be fearful and anxious about asserting themselves, frequently feeling unworthy of love, success or happiness.

Such a father doesn't want their daughters to grow up or become independent as that means losing narcissistic supply. They will do anything to keep you small and make you believe you can't take care of yourself, so naturally, every attempt to be your own person and grow up will be discouraged and sabotaged. Nothing matters more than staying in control and nothing matters less than how you feel and what path you'd like to follow. One survivor I talked to had a father who would constantly criticize her for spending money and not becoming independent like all her peers. And yet, every time she attempted to break free and become independent, her father would say she is not capable enough, mature enough and that she won't be able to do it on her own without family financial support. This mind game not only diminishes all efforts of authenticity, but it also ensures a stable narcissistic supply - *You depend on me, so I will make sure you feel bad about it, and yet I will sabotage every effort you make in trying to be self-reliant.* A narcissist, just like in all other areas of life, has an idealized image of how they want to be treated, and in a family environment this means they want to be the ones everyone worships, listens to and respects.

They want a perfect family they think they deserve, where their daughters fit the image of daughters from Hollywood movies, who are sweet, humble, nicely dressed, don't rebel against norms or their father's expectations. If your father wanted you to be a feminine, nice behaving lady, and you happened to be the artistic type with your own fashion sense, they probably would make sure you feel horrible about the way you look. Narcissistic fathers keep their daughters small, by putting them down, discouraging them and dismissing anything that deviates from their own perception of how a daughter *should be*. Anything that represents an expression of individuality, be it physical looks, personal beliefs, opinions, interests, ambitions, emotions or goals, is seen as unwanted, unacceptable and disrespectful. Choices are not allowed. Any form of normal, healthy desire to express oneself causes the narcissistic father to act passive-aggressive, to rage, ignore, dismiss or punish you.

Dating and socializing is another area of scrutiny, as every person who threatens to take away their narcissistic supply is perceived as a threat and needs to be eliminated. Such fathers either criticize any relationships their daughters have or act uninterested in their social life until the daughter does something that defies the narcissist's code of behavior, which is when the punishment takes the form of forbidding or sabotaging their daughters right to socialize or date. Choosing a group of friends, dating, let alone moving out and living with your partner, are out of the question. Additionally, narcissistic fathers may raise their daughters to distrust men in general. Every man, except their father, is a threat, wants to use them, abuse them and take something away, and while daughters of narcissistic fathers may grow up thinking that men are not to be trusted, they are raised by a real abuser. Frequently, she may even end up with narcissistic, toxic and abusive men which makes her father's prophecy come true. What these women fail to realize, until later in life during their healing journey, is that these are patterns their father taught them and so they seek the same kind abusers their father was, not knowing the real root of toxic relationships they engage themselves in.

Many daughters grow up thinking their fathers wanted to protect them and keep them safe, where in reality, what they discover as they grow up is that the only thing their fathers wanted is to feel important, in control and validated themselves. They wanted a pat on the shoulder from others for how good of a job they did raising their girls, and they wanted to be perceived as the authority they believed they are. These daughters are more often than not prone to harsh self-criticism, self-sabotaging and self-blaming behaviors later in life. One daughter of a narcissistic father I had a chance to meet struggled with anorexia and depression, as her father pushed her to be a model from the age of thirteen. She wasn't allowed to play volleyball as that wasn't very feminine and won't flatter her body, which is one of many examples that speaks to how toxic and destructive being raised by someone who has NPD really is. That is something we will dive more into in the chapter that follows.

Narcissistic father-son relationship

While their little girls are manipulated under the narcissist's parole *I am your protector, I will keep you safe from harm*, their boys are raised in a different manner. Projection, in the case of father-son relationships, becomes even more visible, as the son is not only the person who can make his father look great, but he is also the object onto which the narcissistic father rejects his masculinity and every masculine trait he sees in himself. His desire to dominate, win, gain power, success, and recognition get a more aggressive expression in relation to his son.

Because, in his mind, a narcissistic father's genius and talent are not recognized, he wants his son to prove to the outer world that he, his blood, is the powerful genius he believes himself to be. In other words, he projects his grandiosity and lives through his son, wanting his own child to be a living example of his narcissistic grandiose ideals. He does this by *teaching him how to be a real man*, glorifying overly assertive and pushy behavior, ruthless dominance, rage, anger and other unacceptable ways of acting and relating to others. He encourages his son to push the limits, regardless of how the child feels about it, even inappropriately aggressive and confrontational behavior beyond the child's natural comfort zone and regardless of their temperament. This is a projection, as supporting such behavior reflects the way he himself protects his imaginary authority - through placing his authority upon others and gaining control over them. However, promoting and advocating for behavior does not rely on encouragement, real support and healthy building of the child's self-esteem through collaboration, but on negative emotions and reactions such as fear, anger, rage, guilt, anxiety, stress or blame. He teaches his daughters that he, their narcissistic father, is the ultimate provider and the safe harbor they can trust. He does the same with his sons, but in a slightly different way. He teaches his daughter to fear the exterior world, and their son to hate and feel threatened by the outer world, which is exactly the mixture of emotions he, himself, feels. He portrays other people as a vile competition, an endless tournament where there can be only one winner, which is his son.

Being emotionally distant and unable to empathize, he tries to program his son to discard his own emotions and be ashamed of them, regardless of the child's true affectionate nature. Emotions need to be ignored, suppressed and stand in contrast to masculine roles the narcissist wants their son to take on. Even though the father may have a seemingly emotional bond with his son, this bond usually revolves around negative feelings and represents, just like with other family members, a roller coaster of shame, guilt, and anger versus adoration, glorification, and idealization. A child's true emotions, unless they are a reflection of how the father feels, are dismissed, ignored and if confessed, usually criticized, made fun of or made irrelevant. Ultimately, he wants his son to claim the dominance and recognition in the world he did not succeed in getting – he lives through his son, at his own child's expense. Just like with his daughter, his son's natural talents, temperament, affectionate nature, thoughts and character are not taken into account, and can frequently be harshly criticized. Behind the mask of a father who wants the best for his son - the best career, status recognition, the idea of ideal love - lies a selfish man, who wants to see part of him be revived and get a second chance to earn the alpha male recognition through his son. In relation to women, he may teach his son to disrespect, distrust, take what he needs from them, seduce and use them by telling tales of bad examples and experiences he has had or covertly, by putting his wife down or blaming her for all the upheaval the family has experienced. In his own mind, he is usually the great seducer and charmer and that is what he wants his son to become, as he is his living legacy and an object he lives through and a chance to redeem himself. When the son fails to fulfill his expectations, however, his narcissistic father gets enraged, dismisses, punishes and ignores the child as he himself is living through his son's failure or rejection. *You are weak. You will never become a man. You are a failure. No one will ever respect you. You are a disappointment. You let them win. You let them humiliate you. You are a coward. You let them take the prize.* Instead of offering his child support during challenging times, which he is unable to do, he amplifies the failure as he feels it himself. It is never about his son, but it is about him, as deep down, he has experienced rejection, humiliation or failure and this seriously threatens his enlarged ego and doesn't sit well with his agenda. As a result, the son feels an immense amount of shame, embarrassment, and guilt, and will, as a result, try hard not to disappoint his father again, and by doing so he is giving the father the ultimate narcissistic supply.

Chapter 10:
The effects of paternal narcissism on children

U nfortunately, the devastating effect of paternal narcissism doesn't stop in family, but it expands into adulthood, whether or not there is direct contact with the father. Narcissistic fathers leave a big mark on their children, and so each aspect of their lives mirrors and repeats this unhealthy father-child relationship and learned patterns to an extent. Children who have such a parent can sense the effects of toxic paternal relationships in their friendships, love life, career and life choices. Such upbringing leaves an imprint on one's psyche in a few ways I will talk about below.

Before you start reading, just know this - Your childhood wasn't your choice and the life you are living now is a reflection of the many years of limitation, negative conditioning and mistreatment you have received. If the content below becomes triggering, remember that it is ok to feel the way you feel and to feel triggered. Know that I have felt the same way and that there are other fellow survivors who understand you on a deep level. You may feel like an injustice has been done to you, you may feel life is unfair because you didn't get to choose a better life for yourself when you were younger. You may feel anger or sadness. Whatever you feel, you allow yourself to embrace the feeling. These are natural responses so be gentle with yourself. That is part of your journey and there is nothing shameful or weak about you if you have experienced or are experiencing any of the following effects of being raised by a narcissistic father. Take a deep breath, here we go.

Engaging in unhealthy relationships

Do you feel like your friends and partners are using you?

Do you feel emotionally drained by most people you closely relate to?

Do they make you feel guilty or bad about yourself?

Do you feel like your partners and friends don't care much about you?

Do you feel unloved and unappreciated by them?

If you have found yourself surrounded by friends or partners who used you, were selfish, deceitful or manipulative and you are a child of a narcissistic father, it might comfort you to know that your choice of partners or friends wasn't your fault. Your choice of people is part of your programming and a continuation of the role your father gave you. Here is how.

Children of narcissistic fathers attach their ability to give and receive love to their ability to provide for others, many times not getting the same in return from their partners. Narcissistic fathers make their children feel like whatever they do isn't enough, and so once they reach adulthood, they will stretch themselves too thin in order to maintain toxic, one-sided relationships and friendships. They will crave love the same way they craved it from their father, where nothing was ever enough and they were taken advantage of or unappreciated.

They surround themselves with energy vampires who will always make them feel like what they are giving is not enough They are prone to be gaslighted, frequently in a position where they are taken advantage of, used, abused, manipulated or lied to, because that is the shadow they have been living under their whole life. One feels drawn, repelled and obligated to engage in activities and relationships that don't favor them at the same time and many close interactions reflect the father-child relationship, on more or less conscious levels. Relationships feel like a prison that is hard to escape, yet the prison one continuously puts themselves in is due to the inability to receive love as they were never taught how to. At the end of each relationship, one feels unheard, mistreated, used and abandoned, just like they felt in the family.

Through shame and guilt, two major tools used for programming a child's behavioral responses, the narcissist also creates the predisposition for failed or abusive relationships their children have. These children, including myself, before the healing occurs can find it extremely hard to say no to people. This inability to say no to other people's demands is extremely draining and can create the perfect base for anxiety, frustration, and depression. Because we were taught that living for ourselves and acknowledging our needs is selfish and bad, and because love is conditional and needs to be earned, we would often go out of our way to please other people and put their needs before our own. Furthermore, it may even be difficult to identify, understand and accept our needs, as it is not uncommon to immerse ourselves into other people and merge identities with them, just as we did with our father. This subconscious mechanism drives us to believe that doing things for others, doing favors, salvaging relationships and fighting for them, will bring us love and recognition because we don't know any better. Our worth depends on how well we manage to satisfy other people's demands and respond to their needs, and we may even seek out people who are very dramatic, attention-seeking and demanding as a result of that subconscious need. This way, narcissistic fathers extend their toxicity which continues to take a toll on our mental health. In other words, it is guilt, rather than love that drives most of our relationships until we recognize that we are repeating lessons our father taught us.

Children of narcissistic parents have a belief that if they worked harder at bettering themselves, if they had been a better partner or a friend, and accommodated other people's needs more, they would get a different outcome other than failed relationships. They genuinely think other people's problems are their responsibilities and all upheavals their fault and their burden to carry, while feeling unloved, uncared for and unappreciated by the same people they put before themselves.

While they take on responsibility for every failure in their personal life, they also take the blame that comes with it, and take downfalls as proof that they didn't give their best. They think they always could have done more, while ironically giving their last atoms of strength to cater to other people's needs. Because they were not valued and they spent their whole childhood enabling and providing narcissistic supply, they don't feel valuable unless they are in the role of a caretaker, frequently seeking romantic partners that are unavailable, need help, salvation or to be fixed. More so, they have the compulsion to fix and take responsibility for other people's actions, as they truly believe it is their fault if the relationship goes wrong.

The place in other people's lives is not given freely, but needs to be earned by investing and trying hard to make it work, even if the other party isn't giving back the same effort, or is even abusing this caretaker quality. One's value is directly linked to their ability to fix and change someone or win their love by trying hard and going above and beyond for them. In reality, people they engage with are hardly ever changing and the child of a narcissist will see rejection and failure as their own fault and the proof that they, after all, are not loveable.

Mental health problems

Are you struggling with depression?

Do you feel anxious and paralyzed with fear without knowing why?

Do you find it hard to participate in your own life?

Does your mood change unexpectedly and without warning?

Do you feel distant from yourself or feeling emotionally numb?

The hardest to deal with and the most dangerous effects paternal narcissism leaves on children is depression, eating disorders, anxiety, panic attacks, and different phobias. While depression and other mental health problems can happen to anyone, being raised by a narcissistic father can create a much more solid foundation for mental health issues to occur. Children of narcissistic fathers frequently battle with mental health issues and may display avoidant behaviors and phobias connected to the way they relate to people and their immediate environment. Constant uncertainty, emotional detachment and gaslighting, followed by a clouded identity, create space for the mind of the child to turn to defense mechanisms and behavior patterns.

Because the emotional self was restricted and emotions weren't heard or allowed to be expressed, a child of a narcissistic father may develop different affective disorders. We are taught that emotions mean weakness, they are unjustified and unacceptable and so we spend a lot of mental energy trying to be strong when we are not, which ultimately leads to trouble with intimacy, opening up and eventually breaking down. We reject, disrespect and diminish our emotions just as our father did. These suppressed emotions pile up and the desire to be loved and heard becomes a deep craving and a desire that seems impossible to achieve. Many of us are deeply sensitive individuals, deeply empathetic and emotional, which was not only turned against us, but continues to be a struggle if we keep rejecting that part of us, which many of us do until we start healing. Through completely invalidating the child, a narcissistic father creates an ideal plot for developing depression, which is directly connected to an overbearing sense of unworthiness, lack of self-love and lack of love received. This is a sad but natural response to continually not being seen and heard and living under constant pressure to be better in order to earn love. Depression arises as a result of narcissistic parenting as a whole. Since a child's feelings and needs were unacknowledged by primary caretakers and providers, and they weren't given the tools to recognize their own needs, as adults these children can feel emotionally fatigued, numb and dissociated from one's own emotions until the issue is addressed. They may find themselves unmotivated, drained, unable to cope with the world around them and in need of isolation.

Many children also suffer from anxiety as early as in kindergarten, which continues to follow them through the teenage years and later in adulthood. They were raised to be confused, repressed and were controlled from an early age which creates an inner conflict in a child as it is unable to express itself without inhibition and live in alignment with its true self because they are judged at home for it. When we are not cherished for who we are, we feel abandoned and unworthy, like somehow we don't matter, which is exactly how a narcissistic father makes their child feel.

Children of narcissistic fathers, regardless of sex, may develop sadistic or masochistic behavioral patterns, unconsciously seek pain and involve themselves in situations that don't benefit them, which further, in their mind proves their unworthiness. They may struggle with substance abuse and eating disorders and others may develop antisocial behaviors. There are cases, especially with the scenarios of golden children, where a child may become a narcissist themselves or exhibit some narcissistic traits. Being constantly put on a pedestal and given special treatment makes them believe that they are truly special and so they may seek the same validation they had from their father upon reaching adulthood. They may adopt narcissistic traits of their father and find themselves scapegoats, recreating scenarios from their childhood.

Self-doubt

Do you second-guess yourself?

Do you dwell on the past and judge yourself harshly for not doing better?

Do you constantly feel stuck in life, finding it hard to make a decision?

Constant gaslighting leaves marks and living in a constant state of numbness, being unable to go with the flow of life, second-guessing one's intuition and perception are just some of these marks. People who were raised by a narcissist commonly struggle with self-doubt, which reflects not only in their relationship with the father and family members, but transpires in other areas of life as well. The inability to trust oneself and one's own judgment makes it difficult for those people to make even the simplest decisions. Big life decisions such as choosing a college major, moving places or getting married are areas where one feels unsafe, simply because there is a lack of self-assurance and a fear of making the wrong decision. The narcissistic father usually was the one trying to impose his will onto the child and in adulthood, this creates a blockage to perceiving what feels right, what is good or bad for one's well-being. Even when a decision is made, there is a tendency to dwell on it and second-guess the choice made, especially if prior to choosing a certain direction one pops into an obstacle or a temporary setback. These setbacks are human, but someone who was raised by a narcissistic father may see them as fatal and an ultimate proof that the decision they have made is wrong.

There is a constant inner battle that takes away a lot of mental and emotional energy. You may feel constantly stuck, not knowing which way to go and not trusting yourself enough to make the decisions for yourself. There was always someone who knew better for you, so it is hard to believe that you are perfectly capable of making choices for yourself. If your father is a narcissist you may find yourself constantly swinging back and forth between decisions, not knowing what you truly want. As bizarre it may sound to others who came from healthier family environments, for someone like you and me, knowing exactly what we want can be immensely difficult. Children of narcissistic fathers frequently feel stuck between a rock and a hard place, while not knowing exactly what the rock and the hard place are. There is an extreme amount of mental pressure to make the right choice and so we may be trapped in paralysis for a very long time. The "I wish I had done that or didn't do this" thought creates a vicious circle of regret and feeds the self-doubt, expanding it even more.

The inability to love oneself

Do you think you are complicated or hard to love?

Do you expect perfection from yourself?

Have you ever thought something is wrong with you?

While self-love comes naturally to those who grew up in healthy families, when a family has a narcissist and he happens to take the main role as the head of the household, a child feels from a very young age that they are somehow strange and different from other kids, especially when they have a role of the scapegoat. Since the love they received was always conditional, they don't understand how self-love feels, believing it must be earned by accomplishing one's goals and dreams, just like the love they receive from other people is. The image of themselves their father has created lives in their subconscious, and so children of narcissists fail to see, recognize and love their talents and their own worth. I have encountered so many of them who are beyond successful and have a life many would envy them for, and yet they don't love themselves, they don't love their lives and don't celebrate their success. This is because they don't know how to. They believe that to be truly happy means to be perfect - to believe one is worthy, one needs to achieve incredible success and prove themselves to be extraordinary. Being human is not enough. Ironically enough, this *never good enough complex* creates blockages for pursuing goals that one truly cares about, while they may find themselves making other achievements relatively easy. This goes back to their father's conditioning, where one side of a child's personality was praised and the other dismissed. As a result, the dismissed part of the self can't be fully expressed and not only that - it is followed by a disbelief in one's abilities to achieve what makes their heart sing. Some are so sadly scared of failing and disappointing themselves and their family that they don't even try to pursue certain goals, which keeps them stuck for a long time.

Lack of self-love creates another loop of negative patterns, which is the loop of self-sabotage and self-blame in adulthood. I have been told countless times by my closest friends that they wish they could make me see myself the way they see me. Children of narcissistic fathers don't believe they are anyone special, and may even think everyone else is way better than them, someone who is even doing much less than they are, simply because they weren't recognized in their family as such when they were children. They not only find it hard to trust in their abilities and talents, but they find it hard to believe their own judgment. Learning how to follow the inner guide we all have is difficult, but it is even more difficult if you were raised by a narcissistic parent. Narcissistic fathers are harshly and unjustly critical and need to be in control of their children's lives. This leaves very little space for freedom of expression and thought and a lot of space for self-doubt and even self-hate. If you always see yourself in a negative light, feeling stuck in life while unable to move, this is because your parents failed to give you a valid prize and acknowledge your achievements. Many of us who had toxic upbringing fail to battle the nagging feeling of unworthiness, but that does not prove that we are actually, truly unworthy.

Unclear identity

Do you find it hard to identify and understand yourself and your needs?

Does your life feel directionless?

Do you find it hard to define who you are?

Do you feel like your identity is constantly in a crisis?

Do you feel like you don't fit in or belong anywhere?

Unclear identity is notable both in social interactions and set of personal beliefs. What comes naturally to other children may be postponed for those who were raised by a narcissistic father. You may feel as if you are endlessly floating in life. The real you was suppressed so it is natural that it is difficult to fit in and find out who you are. Your goals may frequently change. If you had goals, you may find that they don't satisfy you, which leaves a sense of emptiness. A lack of meaning and direction in life is frequent for those who were raised by narcissistic fathers, as their identity and the inner child never got a chance to be accepted and nourished. Things you did for a long period of time may not be as fulfilling and you may feel clueless as to who you are and what you want. While others stroll through life following its natural flow, children of narcissistic fathers spend a lot of mental energy trying to figure out what they want and who they are. They feel lost, struggle with a sense of belonging anywhere and may feel deeply dissatisfied about their lives, even if on the outside everything seems to be smooth sailing for them. It is not uncommon for them to feel rejected by social groups, to feel uncomfortable in their own skin and among groups. Troubles socializing, associating with others and social anxiety are some of the ways a lack of clear identity blocks one from living a fulfilling authentic life. If they were compared to other children from a young age, as adults they may continue this unhealthy habit, thinking everyone else is better than them, associating with people with troublesome backgrounds or friends who are approved by their father. Some avoid social interactions altogether due to a sense of personal imperfection and inadequacy. Others may develop social chameleon traits trying to adapt, again, due to lack of clear identity, as one does not know who they are so they may find it difficult to associate with others in an authentic manner.

You were told who you are and you were given a role, so once you are old enough to make your own choices you don't know how to free yourself from the projected ideals and given identity you took on for so long. This is a subconscious process, as we are made to believe that somehow who we truly are is something to be ashamed of and something that needs to stay in control, as no one is going to love us if we display these traits that are authentic to ourselves.

We all have the inner compass that guides us, but in this case, that compass was metaphorically taken away from us, so we could be easier to manipulate into fulfilling a destiny that is not ours to fulfill. Anger, frustration and the nagging feeling like you are running out of time are all connected to harsh conditioning and limitations you as a child received. It is very difficult for children of narcissists to understand exactly what they want, as the expectations and the pressure that was inflicted on them is in direct opposition with what the child truly desires and wants from day one. Their peers may look at them as clueless or confused, which furthermore deepens the wound their father created. Scapegoats are not the only ones who struggle with an identity crisis. Golden children too have an unclear self-image, wondering why people are not always recognizing their talents, as they were raised to believe they are special. These individuals are finding it immensely hard to be in sync with their true identities as they weren't given a chance to separate themselves from the parenting they received. What they do may seem like success and the life they live may seem fulfilling, but because they unconsciously embrace the role they were given as children, many end up feeling lost and depressed because of this inner conflict that perpetually pulls them in two different directions.

Negative self-talk

Do you feel like a failure?

Do you frequently give in to inner criticism?

Do you dwell on past mistakes and failures, while failing to give yourself credit for the success you achieved?

Do you feel like whatever you do is never good enough?

I know how it feels, I have been there. Being constantly blamed for everything that happens in your family and for things that are beyond your control results in constant-self-blame in adulthood. *I can't do this. I am not talented enough. Everyone hates me. I can never find happiness. I don't have what it takes to land that job. I am not attractive enough to find love. I am too sensitive. It is my fault that didn't work out. If I only tried harder.* You name it. Children are selfless and they are like sponges, whatever they are surrounded by they absorb. When that something is negative and blocks their growth, it soon becomes the unconscious pattern of negative self-talk we are frequently unaware of. What we are told is wrong with us becomes what we personally think needs to be fixed. We believe we are not good enough the way we are and that somehow we don't deserve all the good things in life. We believe that people who are happy must be special or somehow better than us because our parents, the father and his flying monkeys failed to be our guide and help us navigate our personal development in a healthy manner. Constantly suppressed feeling of unworthiness creates a loop of negative thoughts, as one believes they are not good enough, successful or attractive enough, seeing themselves in a negative light even when that is far from truth.

Developing a negative self-talk is a very natural response to paternal narcissism. Every conviction we had about ourselves as children internalizes and finds ways to sabotage our happiness in the future. Our father speaks through us even once we break ties with him. These false beliefs we have about who we are, how good and lovable we are, are deep-rooted and we may or may not be aware of them. Because we believed as children that we are somehow not enough the way we are, we tend to develop harsh inner critics and perfectionism, which together threaten to do even more damage to our mental health.

We strive to be perfect and achieve grandiose goals, we overwork and take a lot of burdens to carry along the way while not giving ourselves credit for all the hard work we have done and even criticizing ourselves for not doing better. Negative-self talk is based on false beliefs and we are usually not aware of why we feel the way we do. And that is ok.

Social withdrawal and feelings of inadequacy

Do you feel alone in this world?

Are you deeply afraid of rejection and take criticism to heart?

Do you feel like you are not good enough to be accepted by others?

Do you feel frequent need to isolate yourself from others?

Feeling inadequate is common for us who were ignored and mistreated as children. The treatment we received from our father and our family in general leaves us feeling like outcasts. Being rejected, dismissed and discarded by those who were supposed to love us selflessly creates a belief system that is hard to shake in teenage years and in adulthood. What was once criticism and a blame game at home becomes a fear of being abandoned, rejected and judged by others when we are older. The trick to this pattern of thoughts is that we truly believe we are less than good and that something is inherently wrong with us. We try to be perfect and do our best, and so we become highly sensitive to criticism and take rejection far harder than other people do. Being rejected your whole life is something not many understand as there is a premise that family, just because you have one, is a safe and a healthy place where you can feel the most like yourself. People forget that sometimes it is our fathers who teach us to be submissive and obedient instead of building our self-confidence. If they fail to secure the base for our emotional and mental growth, later in life we may frequently experience feelings of embarrassment, shame, rejection or humiliation. The world can feel just as harsh and unloving as our father was, may leave us just as confused as he did, simply because we were manipulated and controlled from a very young age.

Many who struggled with narcissistic mistreatment in childhood frequently have a desire to hide away from the world and withdraw into a shell where no one can hurt or betray us. This shell is a protective mechanism we subconsciously created for self-preservation when we were children, and in adulthood, even when we still don't need it, we are scared to leave it behind. It is our safe zone, and because we believed that no one cares for us, we felt unlovable, invisible, inadequate or rejected by our own father we think, in the back of our mind, that the other world is as harsh and critical as he or our family was. Feeling like you don't belong anywhere and a fear that people will reject us is fairly common and a normal response to the parenting style you have received. This happens because of the merged identities and projections narcissistic fathers placed upon us, which cause difficulty in being truly open, sociable and authentic with people around us. Even when we are with people we feel isolated, distant and frequently anxious, which can lead to loneliness, feeling misunderstood and feeling rejected by peers, which is just another way in which our father's narcissism affects us without their direct involvement. Our fathers taught us that being ourselves and expressing our true thoughts, needs and desires is somehow bad or wrong and needs to be under control, and so as we grow up that gets transformed into a fear of rejection and a false belief that we can't be loved and accepted as we truly are. As a result, we struggle with anxiety and without knowing it keep on doing what our father did - we keep his tradition by unconsciously rejecting ourselves. Even those who are surrounded by a lot of people and have many friends and acquaintances, feelings of inner loneliness are still there. We either take on certain identities we believe are acceptable and try to mold ourselves to be someone we feel is acceptable and adequate, or we decide to retreat from the world, feeling deeply rejected. In both cases, we are not being authentic, and as long that feeling stays with us, the fear of abandonment, judgment, and rejection will stay as well.

Rejection and being judged by others is taken as another proof of self-unworthiness, and it is hard to cope with, as all living beings need love and nurturing to blossom. When you are stripped of that early on and it happens to continue later, you feel like moving forward in life is a very hard task. Being isolated and relating to more toxic individuals, as mentioned above, can make the healing process even more difficult, as those who have a very little support system, find it hard to extract all their strength to move forward. Although highly unpleasant and painful, it might comfort you to know that you are not alone in your loneliness because that's how we all have felt at some point or even throughout our whole lives. Again, it is yet another part of your conditioning and not a picture of who you are. Remember that all our relationships with other individuals or groups are just a reflection of our relationships with our fathers and not a reflection of our worth and true selves. We are all likable and we all belong somewhere, it's just that finding a sense of belonging first to oneself through embracing our authenticity, and then embracing people can require detours from our original path and belief system.

Helplessness

Do you feel like you have very little control over your life?

Do you feel tired of trying to be strong and make things better?

Does life feel like a constant battle?

Do you feel like life is against you?

When your father is a narcissist, you are constantly pulled in two directions - one that is natural, true and authentic to you, and a second one which is influenced by his toxic parenting. Because he is the person you are supposed to lean on and rely on for help, just as any child, you may find that you believe his word. As you get older, develop opinions, attitudes and gain more and more independence, you feel more and more pressure without knowing why. The pressure to do something with your life. Pressure to succeed. Pressure to move, make changes and choices for yourself. And yet you feel stuck. You have a life before you and you are immobile and paralyzed. Children of narcissistic fathers often tend to feel as if they are somehow restricted to live their life to the fullest as whatever they do will never bring them favorable results. This is because of the restriction imposed on them and this helplessness is a learned helplessness, which means that it is not the reality, but a sort of mental imprisonment a child has learned to live with. Because the narcissistic father needs validation and a narcissistic supply from the child, they will restrict the child from expressing themselves and sabotage all attempts the child makes to change how they are treated. In a narcissist's eyes, a child's free will is a threat and them changing to accommodate their own child means that they no longer have the control, but it's given to the child and that is something they can't allow.

If they give in to a child's displays of affection for too long, they believe they are somehow giving their authority away. If they punish the child for too long, they are afraid to lose the narcissistic supply, so they may do something to hoover the child back. No matter if the child tries to be more considerate, patient, kind, less fussy with their father or not, the result will always be the same - the narcissistic father will always discard them. They discard because that is how they operate and there is no amount of love that can change that. Unfortunately, when we are young we don't know how narcissists operate. All we know is that whatever we do never seems to bring us the desired result or love we crave and so this discard gets internalized and becomes the feeling of helplessness and hyper-awareness of one's behavior to the point it creates deep anxiety.

We get tired of fighting for approval, better life or love and we get drained. Ultimately, when all this is combined with the fact that whatever the child does seems to never be good enough for their father, it creates a lot of angst and confusion for the child, even causing depression. As a result, they become the adult who feels broken, stuck and unable to make a change in their life. If this seems familiar to you, know that you are not alone in your feeling that whatever they do, no matter how hard you work at something, it is never going to change where you are. Matter of fact, it is a very common theme for us, children of narcissistic fathers. Because we have been controlled and hushed our entire lives, feeling like we have no control over our destiny becomes natural. You may even feel like life happens to you, not for you, and that is completely normal considering the impact your narcissist had in your life. It is and it will always be a narcissist's intention to keep you boxed in so you can obey their wishes and fulfill their ideals. You need to understand, even though you may read otherwise, that feeling of helplessness wasn't a choice you could make. It isn't a choice even now at this moment you are reading this. It is simply a pattern, that, just like other patterns, with patience, time and kindness to yourself can be broken and turned into something beautiful.

Being gaslighted, diminished, humiliated, abused or abandoned creates scars that burn even after we have done some healing. We do not choose our parents and how we are raised, so being critical of yourself for not taking charge of your own life is only going to do more damage. We have been our worst enemies and unconscious flying monkeys of our own father, contributing to our own misfortune. That is something no one deserves, and it is something that is not your fault. The next two chapters are meant to help you break free from your narcissistic father's conditioning, break free from their influence and show you the path to healing you will take at your own pace because you are beyond loveable.

Chapter 11:
Breaking free from a narcissistic father

T he first sign of healing from childhood wounds created by your father is acceptance. Accepting that you cannot change your childhood or your father, that what you have experienced was never your fault and it isn't something that defines you, but most importantly, accepting that your father is a narcissist.

For a very long time I felt immensely guilty for even thinking my father was wrong. I internalized every interaction we had and took on all the blame for our relationship going downhill. I remember thinking I am really selfish and overdramatic for even thinking something is his fault and, maybe if I was a better daughter and could be more flexible, he'd appreciate me more and we'd have less clashes. But here is the thing, that is exactly the pattern we talked about previously. Shifting the blame, where you are the one taking all the guilt and all the responsibility for a relationship gone bad. Then I started gaining more clarity by studying psychology and then educating myself more about narcissism, reading tons of books just like you are reading this one. From that point onwards, things started shifting for me. I find it very interesting that many of us who have dealt with some form of abuse or neglect, particularly if we were raised by narcissists, are interested in psychology. I believe we all have that inner compass that wants to find out the truth because something just feels off and we want to understand why. Self-education is the first step to breaking free from the mental prison your father has put you in. The process may not be easy, but as time goes on you go through all five stages of grief, which are denial, anger, bargaining, depression and finally complete acceptance which brings peace and relief.

Even though we may recognize we were raised by an individual who didn't have our best interest at heart, embracing the truth can be difficult, especially when we are young and still glorifying the father we thought we had, and so denial is a natural response to suspicions that your father is toxic and may not be able to give you the love and support you needed. When people grow up and realize they were raised by a narcissist, once they get into what narcissism is at its core, the first reaction is shock and the *this can't be the truth* mentality. In the beginning we make excuses and reminisce on good memories that still prove we are wrong and that what we have discovered is false. As we engage with our father, if we have the opportunity and start seeing patterns that match with our newfound knowledge, that denial shifts into aggression. We get mad at our narcissistic fathers, mad at our family members for allowing them to manipulate and gaslight us, mad at ourselves for allowing it to continue and mad at the universe for not giving us the loving family to grow up in. I remember I felt a sense of huge injustice being done to me. I was angry that unlike my peers who grew up in healthy families, I had to struggle with issues that very few of them relate to. I was angry about being in a position where I needed to heal, instead of enjoying life and being carefree. Nowadays I am glad for the lessons I have learned and I am proud of myself for getting where I am today and being proud of myself was rare when I was younger. You may shift from denial to anger, back and forth and this is called bargaining. Trying to find excuses because what you have discovered is a shock and a huge plot twist on your whole life. Once these inner battles are over, you may feel depressed and hopeless, so everything you were angry about turns into deep prolonged sadness. We have all been there and you are not alone. However long it takes, give yourself the time to grieve your childhood, and feel as angry, depressed or confused as you need to.

When the whirlpool of emotions goes away, everything falls into place. You realize you are not crazy. You haven't imagined things. There is an explanation to what you have been experiencing your whole life. Something that didn't feel right, but was hard to explain and rationalize now has a name - narcissistic personality disorder. Suddenly, you stop feeling as guilty for being an ungrateful child as you used to. It doesn't happen overnight, but the heavy weight of guilt slowly fades away as you gain more clarity. It is called acceptance.

One of the first signs that you are breaking free from your father and his impact on you is that you start not only understanding narcissism but recognizing it in people. This may bring you a sense of unsafety and even paranoia, as you may think the whole world is full of narcissists who are out to get you. This is also the first step to breaking free from long-term effects your father had on your behavior and relationship patterns, as you start eliminating toxic people from your life solely for recognizing the signs of narcissism. You clear the air and start saying no to people, but most importantly, you start understanding the role you have been playing all along, the role you had in your family that colored in all other relationships you had. Your narcissistic father may have sabotaged you in many areas, but his narcissistic ways have made you ten times more resilient and aware of your surroundings than people who did not have the chance to be raised by a dysfunctional parent. Whether you like it or not, you will be much more aware of how the human mind works, much more alert to sociopathic, psychopathic and other abnormal human behaviors and patterns that go with that. This also means that you will be much less prone to relationships with such individuals, which is a real blessing in disguise, as it will lead you to much healthier, more positive and nourishing relationships than you had in the past. This way, learning about your father's patterns and narcissism, in general, will set you free from his influence in future relationships.

The newfound clarity is the stepping stone for breaking free from your father's control and from the conditioning you unconsciously embraced. Knowing that you were raised by a mentally unhealthy individual is a hard pill to swallow, but it will help you limit or completely cut the contact with him. The best way to deal with all narcissists is to detach yourself, emotionally, mentally and physically, as much as you can. Cutting contact or keeping it to a minimum is the ideal scenario. However, in cases when you still live with your parents or you don't have the option to retreat from an unhealthy environment, the very clarity and knowing of who you are dealing with will help you see the relationship dynamically differently. You will notice that you are not as worried as you used to be about whether or not you will hurt their feelings and you will start to feel less guilty for doing things that are good or right for you. Knowledge and self-education will help you see your father from a new, more detached angle which will in turn give you more space to breathe. Now you know they want to control you and you are prepared for manipulation, accusations and gaslighting. Staying in touch with your father and your family requires a lot of self-awareness, and so if you are in contact, never forget who you are dealing with.

Narcissistic fathers will try to influence your life no matter how old you are and they will try to hoover you, blame you or dismiss you just as they did in the past. However, the difference between your childhood and adulthood will be that now you know how to successfully recognize his narcissistic patterns of behavior and therefore you will be able to observe it rather than react to it. If you are in contact, keep your privacy to yourself. Unfortunately, narcissistic parents use the trust their child has in them to manipulate and control the outcomes of their child's behavior. Staying private about your life will give them less material to use against you and less space to interfere with your life and decisions. Being distant and knowing you have to keep your greatest joys secret from your family may be sad, but it is unfortunately crucial to keeping your sanity most of the time.

You will notice that how you perceive the world around you changes. These changes in perception will lead you to a new life, where you love yourself, trust yourself and your abilities and most importantly - feel free. Something you have struggled your whole life with will slowly start to dissolve and the next chapter will be all about that - embracing your wounds, reparenting yourself and becoming your own creator.

Chapter 12:
Steps to healing and rewriting your story

F inding out your father is a narcissist is not easy, and the imprint his parenting style has created may seem hard to break free from. You may feel blocked from your own destiny, unable to live your life the way you desire. We have all been there and we all go back there unwillingly from time to time, and that is ok. Matter of fact, it is completely normal. You are not a machine and there is no magic button to turn off your subconscious mind that keeps repeating your father's words. This very moment as you are reading this, I want you to give yourself the credit for trying to learn about your father, your upbringing and why you feel so blocked or lost. It takes an immense amount of courage and desire to change your circumstances for the better and to get to the point where you can say I am a child of a narcissistic father and accept that. Complete acceptance, as mentioned earlier, is the first step and probably the hardest leap to take. Know that learning is never linear and start your healing journey gently and with patience.

Everything starts with your *enough is enough, I am not tolerating being mistreated anymore. I don't deserve this treatment I am receiving and I want to be happy for a change.* If you are looking for ways to heal, it is likely that this is exactly what you have thought. This is a great sign as it means that you are stepping into your power, even if you still feel down, stuck or ashamed. While you may feel like this internally, it can be difficult to assert these thoughts and make them a reality, but with practice, learning self-love and other techniques, it becomes easier over time. Understand that some people will not be able to understand you, so don't feel discouraged if that happens. Someone who hasn't experienced narcissistic abuse from their father may be able to relate to your experience and that is ok. What matters is that you understand and relate to your experience.

Below are some of the techniques you can use to understand yourself, eliminate negative behavioral patterns that have been reinforced by your father for a long time, and then slowly replace them. Hopefully, these will give you helpful insight, enlighten your journey and lead you towards unconditional self-love.

Developing emotional intelligence

Being raised in a healthy environment creates a predisposition for what your father or people around you may have labeled you as, oversensitive. If you can describe yourself as being too emotional, too sensitive or unstable, know that first, you are not alone in that feeling, and two, the range of emotions you feel show great capacity for empathy and emotional richness not many people possess. Matter of fact, your narcissistic father may have chosen you for the role you played precisely because of your ability to empathize and feel things on a deep level. That being said, your predispositions for developing emotional intelligence are already there, so what you need to do is just find a way to swim in those emotions in a way that is natural and healthy for you. Developing emotional intelligence is about you learning that it is ok to feel, not to reject and be embarrassed about your own emotions. We all tune in to different frequencies, but people like you and me, in particular tend to be very, even hyper-aware of things around us, which causes constant emotional alertness and intense emotional reactions. This is something to be honored. Once you honor emotions, don't think about them, but instead feel them as organically as you can. We were taught to repress or be ashamed of feelings, so the important step to healing is embracing them and for many of us, learning to recognize them for what they are. Feeling and recognizing your emotions for what they are, instead of thinking them or judging yourself for feeling a certain way, is half the job done. When you know what it is that you are feeling, you can then safely find ways to manage your own responses in a way that is not limiting to you, without self-censoring or blame. Your emotions don't define you but are only your response to the experiences you have and are all human.

Counseling with a therapist, meditating, practicing mindfulness and journaling can be ways that can help you on this journey. Remember that healing an emotional body can be one of the toughest tasks, but accepting and then slowly diminishing the effects of shame, guilt and resentment is possible and it does happen when we become friends with this very important part of our beings - our feelings.

Coming to terms with your upbringing

Healing begins once you start acknowledging that your childhood is only a part of your path and not the determining element of your future. I used to see my childhood as an unfair disadvantage that held me back in life. I used to blame my father and held a lot of resentment towards him because of the way he raised me, sabotaged my growth and happiness. To a large extent, that was true, but I allowed myself to stay in the energy of anger and resentment for too long, which adds only prolonged healing and amplified negative effects that my father's narcissism created for me. You cannot change the past and you should not put the pressure on yourself to do better in the present if you still feel resentful or held back by your family history. It seems very unfair to be stripped of the basic support system and to be discarded by your own father, and even more unfair that you have to embark on the healing journey before you start to live the life you want. But that is your journey.

Accept where you came from and understand that the trials and tribulations your father put you through had nothing to do with you, your worth or how lovable you are. You don't have to forgive your father or your family for mistreating you or neglecting you, but you absolutely need to forgive yourself and see your family life as a tough journey you will come out on the top from. It is part of you and please be proud of yourself for playing whatever role you were given for so long, because it takes a lot of resilience and inner strength, to be able to do that. Enduring the narcissistic treatment from your own father is a sign of fortitude, so don't reject it, but rather stand tall. You have been through it all and yet here you are, reading this book, facing your demons and your past, trying to find your way out and through. That is courage. You were a threat to your father's sense of power, not because you are weak, but because you are powerful, so accept where you came from and own it.

Strengthening the identity

Because you were told who you should be from day one of your life, defining who you are can be a tricky task, simply because even though you may have developed interests and beliefs, it is likely that there are some that you have unconsciously adopted. These would be choices, beliefs, ideals, and ideas that you live by and have taken on, but you find them not to be as satisfying. These beliefs are those we have about ourselves and the world around us that don't serve us. Many are created as defense mechanisms, while others are incorporated in our system without us consciously being aware of them. You may feel confused about which way to go in life and that is ok. Maybe you always wanted to become an artist, but you were made to believe that you won't be successful at it, so you may have suppressed that part of your identity and refocused your attention to something your father thought was more useful. Maybe you wanted to express yourself through dressing a certain way or living an alternative lifestyle. Whatever your story may be, to heal from narcissistic damage caused by your father you need to get in touch with who you truly are. What is it that you always wanted to do but didn't because you were afraid of failure, judgment or rejection? Your father has used these fears to guide you in the direction that suits them and enables their narcissistic supply, so you need to embrace those fears and understand who they come from. It is ok to be yourself. Let go of fear and whenever you are about to do something, start asking yourself:

Will it make me happy?

Do I feel expansive when I am doing this?

Do I want to feel this way?

What will happen if I do what I feel called to do?

Do I feel like myself when doing this?

Is this really what I think or is it my father speaking through me?

How will I feel if I accept/reject this offer? Why?

Knowing who you are means rediscovering and finding lost pieces of yourself and putting the puzzle back together. The stronger the bond you have with your authentic self, the less power your narcissistic parent will have over you. Take your time to find these answers then strengthen the bond with the person you find on the other side - yourself. Please stop judging your real self, because that is what your father did for so long.

Our experience with narcissistic fathers can be very different, so strengthening the core of your identity may be different than mine and vice versa. This can vary from learning more about who you are to completely rediscovering yourself and finding your true self. Be patient with yourself, discover yourself bit by bit and things will slowly start falling into place.

Developing positive self-talk

Replacing the *I am worthless, I will never make it, I am unlovable with I am worthy, I will make it and I am lovable* is something that takes practice, but it is achievable. Positive self-talk is based on self-love, which develops through acts of kindness to ourselves. It is when you start to matter to yourself more than someone's opinion, judgment or criticism does. It is about accepting yourself just the way you are because you are perfectly fine that way.

Practicing positive self-talk is also based on turning negative experiences into positive lessons by reversing your perception. This is possible particularly for us who were raised by narcissistic fathers, as their narcissism, whether we know it consciously or not, has helped us develop certain traits that are actually great virtues and strengths. If your father is a narcissist, you are likely very observant, curious, empathetic, hard-working and resilient. This alone makes you very capable, which is likely now how you'd describe yourself. This is because you were programmed to think your virtues are your flaws, because these virtues were twisted as they were too overbearing for your narcissistic father to deal with. Instead of praising your hard work and dedication, you were made to believe that what you are doing is average, or they may have even called you lazy. If you are observant or curious, they would say you are wasting time, call you suspicious or nosy. These are just some examples meant to show you how the way our father talked to us finds its way into adulthood and creates a loop of negative self-talk. Instead of your father calling you lazy, now you call yourself that, even when you are just taking a well-deserved break. The path to healing is understanding this, taking a moment to listen to your inner talk and then learning to stop yourself in repeating what your father has made you believe about yourself. What you need to understand, which is not easy for us kids of narcissistic fathers is that failures and mistakes don't define us. More so, they are not a validation that we aren't good enough.

Would you like someone to call you stupid, lazy, incompetent or unattractive? You absolutely would not. Even if someone calls you these names, why would you do that to yourself? You cannot control your father or anyone else, and therefore they don't have the power to tell you who you are and how good you are. They are not you, they are not in your body and they will never be. You have you. So be gentle to that person you see in the mirror, they have been through a lot and they don't need yet another negative comment from the person looking back from the other side of the glass.

If you were raised in a negative environment, building a negative image of yourself is natural. Narcissistic fathers focus on flaws and fail to give praise, so that is what we embrace ourselves. When we grow up we see only the failures, the mistakes, the bad choices and how we can never measure up to the ideals we expect from ourselves. We are so used to the negativity that we forget to see the little good things. We brush off compliments. Developing positive self-talk means reversing whatever is it that your father made you believe. Accepting and enjoying compliments and your own accomplishments. Giving yourself credit for the things you did. Put the pause on perfectionism. You don't need to be perfect to be loved. You don't need to be extremely successful to be respected, heard or seen. These are all fears projected by your father and not a reality, as you are absolutely fine and lovable just the way you are. Take the time and be compassionate with yourself as you would be with someone in need.

Choosing yourself

If you were invisible to your father and your family, you may grow up being invisible to the most important person in your life - yourself. To heal we first need to deal with our inability to say no without feeling guilty. Narcissistic fathers discourage acts of self-love and self-care as they need their children to cater to their narcissistic needs. This is why to break free it is important to learn to clearly recognize our own needs and then prioritize them. You are probably very familiar with the guilt you feel for saying no to other people's demands. As a result of being raised by a narcissist and in a dysfunctional family, we learned to be providers, caretakers, nurturers and that is the role we took on for a long time, giving the energy to people who most likely didn't deserve it. The key to healing here is reversing the focus on ourselves without feeling like we have to apologize for doing something that is good for us. You choose yourself by setting boundaries and making your own codex of behavior, the things you'll tolerate and the things you won't. Healthy boundaries will additionally push away the people who are selfishly using you and taking from you without giving back, and draw in healthy people who respect those boundaries because they respect you and your energy.

Establishing boundaries and asserting them works like a muscle. The first few times you get sore, aka you feel immensely guilty for not responding to someone and catering to their needs, but the more you do it, the better you will feel. Start small and reject invitations or requests that take your energy at the given moment. The guilt you have is coming from being ashamed of having needs because that is what your father found suitable. To have a peaceful, joyous and quality life, and to genuinely give to others, you first need to care for yourself. Every time you feel guilty for not following your gut instinct and extending yourself beyond personal limits to be there for others, remember to take a step back and put yourself first - the person who is asking for your help, energy or favor, no matter who they are, is doing the same. Ask yourself, do you do favors because you genuinely care or because deep down you want to avoid unpleasant feelings of guilt and shame? Know that there is nothing shameful about caring for yourself. It is not your responsibility to make someone else happy or miserable. They are responsible for their own wellbeing, just like you are responsible for yours. Your needs are just as valid as someone else's, no matter how bad they seem to be doing. So don't forget to choose the caring person who is always there for others over anyone else - always chose you.

Re-parenting yourself

I remember I believed for a very long time that had I been given the caring, love and nurturing in my family I would be in a much better place in life. That is true to an extent, because while our upbringing does influence how we carry ourselves through life, it isn't the determining factor, even if it doesn't seem like it at all at this very moment. Your original upbringing has caused wounding, so to heal you must re-parent yourself. Re-parenting yourself means reaching your inner child, embracing it and then teaching it love instead of fear. We are afraid we are not good enough. We are afraid we are not talented, attractive or successful enough. We are afraid we are not lovable. These fears stemmed from the treatment we received as children and the roles we took in our father's hierarchy of importance and worthiness. What can help is visualizing yourself as a child, seeing your fears, tears you have cried and how you felt. Once you can do that, the next step is treating yourself as you always wanted to be treated by your father and your family. Every time you feel anxious, sad or afraid, imagine yourself as a child. How would you comfort that child? By ignoring, judging, criticizing for screaming at it like your father did, or by making it feel safe, giving it consolation, and unconditional affection? Re-parenting yourself includes taking a step back from how you were raised, taking on and reversing the role of your dysfunctional father and giving yourself everything you needed from him, be it acceptance, love or kindness. This will include becoming visible to yourself, and treating yourself the way you wanted to be treated. This will not only make you feel safer in your own skin, but it will allow you to accept yourself the way you are, without imposing self-criticism and unrealistic expectations on yourself.

By not rejecting yourself and supporting your inner child and nurturing your vulnerabilities instead of discarding them, you are ultimately taking responsibility for yourself. You could not choose your childhood, but now you can choose yourself and you can become your own person of trust, someone you always needed and who was never there. Please remember that you already have what it takes to re-parent yourself, as otherwise you wouldn't be hoping or looking for healing and you are absolutely not alone. Re-parenting includes an immense amount of self-care and self-nurturing. It also includes getting in touch with your inner child and recognizing it's needs and understanding how it wants to express itself, which goes hand in hand with choosing yourself. Choose you, because you deserve all those beautiful things you were made to believe you are undeserving of.

If you find it difficult to cope with life's challenges and need support, I highly advise seeking the right therapy for you, talking to trusted people if you have them in your life and doing your best to take care of yourself. I want you to know that you are much more than you realize and I hope you will be able to find compassion you always needed as a child deep within yourself.

There is life after a difficult upbringing and your narcissistic father will have less impact on your life with each step you take toward healing. What awaits you on the other side is a shame-free life, a life where you understand guilt rather than internalize it and let it define you. Healing will allow you to see your father from a whole new perspective and most importantly, to see yourself in a much more realistic, positive light.

Conclusion

P aternal narcissism is an illness that impacts not on the person who has it, but more importantly and more significantly everyone else in the family, particularly children. Someone who has not experienced it as a child, will have trouble understanding it, as such fathers are masters of disguise who appear to be the best dads there are, while being immensely toxic for their children and their entire family. It is a sickness that leaves a mark on the offspring that can be hard to deal with in adulthood. The relationship a child has with a narcissistic father is based on manipulation, control, projection and blame games, so it consequently steals joy from the child's life. Narcissistic fathers sabotage freedom and take away the power from their children. Parent-child relationships with them lack in real depth a truly intimate interpersonal connection has, as a narcissist is not able to love unconditionally, but loves only with strings attached.

Narcissistic fathers are everything but protectors, although they know very well how to play that role. They, instead of supporting their child, try to diminish them, discard, ignore and abandon them when the child needs them the most. Instead of helping the child strengthen their self-confidence and personal power, narcissistic fathers prey on their child's weaknesses, as even their own children are seen as a threat to their imaginary authority and grandiosity. Children of narcissistic fathers feel used, abused, unloved and abandoned, many times without knowing why or being able to pinpoint what is it that makes them feel the way they do. This is because their fathers are gaslighting, shifting the blame and projecting, which can be very hard to spot for someone who has no knowledge and awareness of narcissistic behavior. The main damage they do lies in the misuse of their power and role of the father, which they utilize to gain narcissistic supply from their children, the family as a whole and the society.

Children who grew up with them are the ones who were not given the freedom to be children nor the freedom to be themselves. At a very young age there was a role they were demanded to play and anything that deteriorates from that role, even if it is something that makes the child happy, needed to be punished, suppressed and controlled.

The bond between the narcissistic father and their child exists, but it is unhealthy and not based on mutual respect and love, but on shame and guilt. Such a father projects his deepest fears of inadequacies, shame and rejection on their children, but they also do the same for their ambitions, unrealistic qualities, imagined authority and false sense of personal power, grandiosity and success. Based on these two they give their children the roles of the scapegoat and the golden child where the first one becomes the embodiment of the narcissistic fathers' fears and the second one becomes the embodiment of their ideals. Neither of these are based in reality and are never a reflection of a child's real potential, skill, character or talent. The scapegoated child is the one who is ultimately the greatest threat to a narcissist's false sense of self-importance, and so that child will be the one to be discarded and rejected. In homes with more children, his children may easily get abandoned for their siblings simply because they are giving the father a better narcissistic supply, are better at feeding their ego by playing out the ideals their father has, catering to him, adoring and worshiping him. In other words, equality and mutual support are not in a narcissistic father's vocabulary as he makes his children compete for his admiration, love and attention.

139

Narcissistic fathers poison the whole family with this competitive energy and instead of creating a safe environment for the children to grow, they turn family members against each other. The children's mother and the scapegoated child are usually the ones to blame for all the failures, mistakes and wrongdoings, particularly for those he himself has committed. His wife is described as emotionally cold, distant, unloving, unsupportive and a sabotager of his and the family happiness or she takes the role of the flying monkey, catering to his needs, adoring him and supporting his toxic parenting, many times unconsciously.

While part of good parenting includes being able to prevent deviant behaviors in children and raise happy, healthy and assertive individuals, having a father who is a narcissist means purposefully taking advantage of the fatherly role and exerting extreme authoritarianism and control over the children. They are, deep down, extremely vulnerable to rejection and criticism, are resentful and have bottled a lot of shame in a very deep corner of their subconsciousness. Such a father has no empathy, no sensitivity to their child's needs, but is observant enough to spot what these needs are and use them to gain his narcissistic supply. His children are seen as possessions that belong to him, are emotionally neglected, made to be overly codependent on him for affirmation, money or appreciation even in adulthood. Their emotional scope is very narrow and infantile, so their dealings with children are colored with aging and passive-aggressiveness, rather than maturity and openness.

Ultimately, knowing paternal narcissism opens one to perspectives many people are unaware of. While a difficult road, one can heal from the wounding caused in childhood and rise above it. In fact, that is exactly what happens in the great majority of cases for those whose father was a narcissist. It takes patience, kindness to oneself, learning about self-love, self-compassion and self-re-parenting to come out the other end, and it is not a mission impossible. Narcissistic fathers make us feel alone, isolated and rejected, so it is through healing work that we embrace who we are without continuing to do the same thing our father did - judge and criticize ourselves. It is through learning about paternal narcissism, its toxicity and the nature of interpersonal relationships that it influences that we rise above. And in the end, we truly do.

Made in the USA
Las Vegas, NV
07 November 2024

11293734R00079